man
with a
pram

JON FARRY & STEPHEN MITCHELL

man
with a
pram

the bloke's guide
(from conception to birth) to all the stuff
you need to know, do, prepare and pack
for the best moment of your life

hachette
AUSTRALIA

IMPORTANT NOTE TO READERS: Although every effort has been made to ensure that the contents of this book are accurate, it must not be treated as a substitute for qualified medical advice. Always consult a qualified medical practitioner. Please also note that medical information and organisational contact details are subject to change. Neither the authors nor the publisher can be held responsible for any loss or claim arising out of the use, or misuse, of the suggestions made or the failure to take advice.

Every effort has been made to acknowledge and contact the copyright holders for permission to reproduce material contained in this book. Any copyright holders who have been inadvertently omitted from acknowledgements and credits should contact the publisher and omissions will be rectified in subsequent editions.

hachette
AUSTRALIA

Published in Australia and New Zealand in 2010
by Hachette Australia
(an imprint of Hachette Australia Pty Limited)
Level 17, 207 Kent Street, Sydney NSW 2000
www.hachette.com.au

10 9 8 7 6 5 4 3 2 1

National Library of Australia
Cataloguing-in-Publication data:

Mitchell, Stephen (Stephen J.), 1968–
Farry, Jon
  Man with a pram – Stephen Mitchell and Jon Farry.

  1st ed.
  978 0 7336 2505 3 (pbk)
  Includes index.

  Pregnancy – Popular works.
  Pregnant women – Relations with men.
  Pregnant women – Physiology.
  Pregnancy – Psychological aspects.

618.24

Cover design by Design by Committee
Text design by Agave Creative Group
Zooped-up pram artwork by Stephen Mitchell
Typeset in Adobe Garamond by Agave Creative Group
Printed in Australia by Griffin Press, Adelaide, an Accredited ISO AS/NZS 14001:2004
Environmental Management Systems printer

*To Jean and Katina, thanks for all the hard work
on my behalf (JF)*

*To my fantastic wife Sonal, my very cheeky daughter Maya,
and my dear mum, Merle (SM)*

man
with a
pram

contents

Preface

A pregnancy book that men will actually read!

We originally called this book the more macho sounding *The Secret Men's Guide To Pregnancy*, but our hip female publisher argued that the image of a man with a pram was 'hot' and we were unable to concoct an argument against her line of reasoning. Also (just to let you know) the pink title wasn't really our first choice but we couldn't argue our way out of that either!

The idea of this book came from a problem the authors were discussing in a Men's Pregnancy Support Group. OK, admittedly this support *group* was pretty informal and basically consisted of two guys drinking perhaps one too many beers in a pub. The gripe at the time concerned two factors that were weighing heavily on us and becoming a continuing irritation throughout our partners' pregnancies.

The first factor was that there seemed to be an almost total lack of books about pregnancy aimed at men; in retrospect this was probably because no one had been *stupid* enough to try to write one before. The second factor was that both our partners seemed to be showing increasing irritation at our lack of interest in the pregnancy books that they kept strategically leaving around the house. The sub-text of their irritation seemed to be that we (read *men*) were simply not interested in pregnancy and ergo our partners' lives, aspirations and very being in general. An argument which we found to be just a tad unjustified.

Amazingly further 'research' at other Men's Pregnancy Support Groups (with at least two other guys) seemed to confirm a common belief among women on this subject. I mean the nerve! Now it's fairly obvious that men are a bit disconnected from pregnancy as let's face it *they're not actually pregnant*. But it would be a cruel misjudgement to say they wouldn't be interested if the information available was more in tune to their primitive brains.

Female pregnancy books, with their pages full of pictures of inanely grinning people who for some reason are always staring into blank space through a blurry white fog, simply do not appeal to men. They also seem to take a strange tone that makes you feel like they are trying to address someone who is mentally deficient or under five years old. This plus any paragraph that uses the word 'embark', 'journey' or 'adventure' more than three times to describe pregnancy is a sure sedative for the male species. They just switch off: 'Of course I'm interested in the pregnancy honey!' Embark … journey … adventure … SNORE!

We knew what we had to do.

We had to selflessly write a book which appealed to men for the sake of pregnant couples everywhere. It had to be factual, funny, practical, interesting, a bit blokey and somehow appeal to men and women alike with funny facts and interesting tit-bits. It was a hard ask and ironically took ages as we ended up having babies, which take up a lot more time than we suspected, but here it is. We *embarked* on the *adventure*, nay *journey*, and finished the bugger!

1

The Hard Yards
Getting Pregnant Checklist

☑ Have a chat with your partner about which getting-pregnant method suits you best.

☑ Lay off the drink and smokes, and get fit ... let's get those sperm buffed!

☑ Get informed: she'll be impressed if you know what you're talking about.

☑ Talk to your doctor about folic acid supplements – for both her *and* you – before you start trying to get pregnant.

☑ Work on your technique (don't worry, guys, it's nothing tricky).

☑ Put on the ol' Barry White, it's time for some sweet lovin'.

☑ If you have no known health concerns but are not successful in getting pregnant within twelve months, see your doctor.

☑ Most of all ... don't worry; relax – this is meant to be fun!

Picture this: a romantic dinner coupled with a bottle of fine wine, lustful looks exchanged between you and your partner. Later, you stumble into the bedroom and rip off each other's clothes. Your partner erotically checks the calendar for the third time, before seductively testing the viscosity of her cervical mucus between her thumb and forefinger: oh, what a night!

If you're reading this chapter then it's safe to say that your partner isn't pregnant but you're in the process of trying to get pregnant, which means lots of sex (at least at certain times), which should be a good thing. With all this jiggy-jiggy going on you've probably forgotten how the whole thing actually works if you ever knew in the first place! Every time you do the deed your sperm take an arduous and incredible journey through your partner's body, a journey that will hopefully end in a baby in nine months.

Imagine a large city marathon with its 60 000 runners surging up the main street: some of them professional athletes, some dressed in funny costumes, some starting to stumble within the first couple of kilometres, but all of them pounding their way towards the finish line. It's a long and exhausting run. There will be only one winner.

Now imagine that your partner's vaginal passage is the heavily pounded pavement of that same main street, and her fallopian tubes are the winding course of the race. *Now* multiply the number of runners by 5000 and ... actually, let's not go there!

The average number of sperm in a healthy male's ejaculation is around 200–300 million, and like in any marathon there is usually only one winner. All that sperm and only a couple of eggs – odds are pretty damn good, you would think.

In fact, the mechanisms of conception are actually a bit of a lottery, based on timing and the general health of sperm and egg. Added to this, of all those millions of sperm less than 100 000 make it through the cervix, while only a measly 200 or so make it up the fallopian tubes, leaving only one to fertilise the egg (two in the case of fraternal twins, but let's not even contemplate that right now). Looked at this way, if it was a city marathon it would be a *massacre*.

There are three different approaches to achieving the magic bun in the oven. Your basic options are:

1. the relax-and-see-what-happens approach;
2. the active approach;
3. the seek-medical-advice approach.

What decision you make really depends on your attitudes and personal circumstances, but once you have chosen a path, give it a set period of time (say, twelve months), and if it's not working, try a different approach. To assist in your decision making, there are a few things to take into account. They include:

Your general and reproductive health. If you or your partner have a known medical problem that will affect your chances of conception or pose potential problems for the term of pregnancy, or if either of you has a chronic disease, go and see a doctor before attempting to conceive.

Age and fertility. The world is full of women who have developed successful careers and gone on later in life to have equally successful pregnancies. However, statistics from world population data reveal that as a woman gets older, her chance of becoming pregnant and successfully carrying a child through to term starts to decrease.

Familiarity breeds contempt – and children.

Mark Twain

When a woman moves beyond the age of 35 there is an increase in her rate of infertility and a decrease in her ability to carry a baby. The following statistics were collated for the American Society for Reproductive Medicine in 2003.

Maternal age	Risk of infertility	Risk of miscarriage	Risk of chromosomal disorders
35–39	22%	18%	1/192 at 35
40–44	29%	34%	1/66 at 40
45 +	*	53%	1/21 at 45

* When the female partner reaches the age of 45, 87% of couples were infertile. The rates of infertility increase with age until almost 100% of couples were infertile when the female partner reached 49. (*British Medical Journal*, 1987).

Spicing It Up

So, the sex-for-babies business has become a bit of a drag. Tried everything to rev up your love life but nothing seems to be working? Extensive research has come up with two of the more out-there ways to get the fires of passion going again. Read on ... or perhaps just light a few candles instead.

Kokigami

A recent book by Burton Silver and Heather Busch (Ten Speed Press) may be the answer to your bedroom boredom. *Kokigami: Performance Enhancing Adornments for the Adventurous Man* attempts to revive the art of penis origami decoration, apparently all the rage with the ancient Japanese upper classes. The book offers 14 full-colour, DIY cut-outs to enhance your member. These include the Urgent Fire Engine (common in ancient Japan), the Jubilant Cock and the Slobbering Dog.

The idea is that you fit the appropriate character onto your member and, with your partner, go through an erotic act called 'The Play'.

A suggested script for the Graceful Squid runs as follows:

> **The Call:** 'Come to me little fishy. Let my strong sensitive tentacles stroke and enfold your quivering body!'
> **The Reply:** 'Your tentacles dance most beautifully but they have many suckers and I wonder what they are for?'

(Nudge nudge, wink wink. Say no more.)

The *Kama Sutra*

Written by Mallanga Vatsyayana some time between the first and fifth centuries, the *Kama Sutra* is the one-stop Hindu handbook of love-making, designed specially for those who are able to place both feet behind their head with ease.

The text contains a range of advice on kissing, pressing, scratching and biting. (Sounds like fun!) It also divides men and women to three types, according to their 'size', with fairly self-explanatory names: you may be a hare man, a bull man or a horse man, while your partner may be a female deer, a mare or an elephant.

A multitude of positions giving 'ecstatic enjoyment' are described, offering positions such as the crab, lotus, tiger, elephant, boar, cat, dog, horse, ass, cow, tongs, top, swing and splitting bamboo, just to name a few.

A word of warning when using the *Kama Sutra*: have the local hospital's number close at hand, especially if attempting the elephant versus hare, ass position. Many of the positions may require a full paramedic team to separate you and your partner if things go wrong.

While ageing does affect male fertility too, the results are not as remarkable, with men reported to have fathered children in their nineties.

Let's look at the three approaches to getting pregnant in a bit more detail.

1. The Relax-and-See-What-Happens Approach

Life is fraught with stresses – the job, the bills, the mother-in-law – so getting stressed about falling pregnant is something that most couples would like to avoid. With the relax-and-see-what-happens approach, Mother Nature takes command and all you have to do is woo your partner to have sex two or three times a week. Easy! The rationale is that if you are having stress-free sex this frequently, you are likely to match up with your partner's most fertile times anyway.

Statistics from the National Health Service (NHS) in the UK (which Australia sponsors for fertility research) show that about 84 per cent of couples in the general population will conceive within one year, provided they are having regular sex (two or three times a week). The NHS also found that of those who didn't manage to conceive in the first year, approximately half will succeed in the second year, which is a cumulative pregnancy rate of 92 per cent.

So, light up the candles and let Cupid out of that gate! Have sex two or three times a week and see how it goes. How long you want to persist with this method is up to you, but give it a set time and if you haven't fallen pregnant within that period, think about trying the active approach (see below), or visit a doctor together to work out a plan.

2. The Active Approach

Being fairly unique and, let's face it, really lucky, humans copulate for pleasure and reproduction, as opposed to just about all other animals who only have sex at times of female fertility. Cool, huh! Your partner is, in a perfect world, ready to have sex any time of the day, any day of the year – work and social commitments, and the occasional headache, taken into account.

How to Keep Sex For Procreation Fun

It's probably safe to say that this sex-for-baby stuff is a bit different from the sex-for-enjoyment stuff you're used to. Timing, pressure to perform on request and emotional strain can start to make the whole thing somewhat mechanical and, let's face it, a bit of a drag. So it's important to keep a few things in mind when having sex for procreation.

• Keep it romantic.
• Keep up your sense of humour.
• Relax: anecdotal evidence abounds as to couples who stopped worrying and started reproducing.
• Keep having sex outside of fertility times: it takes the pressure off, and keeps it fun. (Remember that?)

So, with all this sex for sex's sake going on, it is sometimes a shock to find out that the fertility window for women is actually relatively small and somewhat unpredictable. The average healthy woman is fertile for only six days out of her (approximately) 28-day cycle. An egg can only survive unfertilised for one day after it is released, while the average sperm can survive for up to four days in the vagina. To complicate things, some women may ovulate earlier or later than expected.

If you are taking this option, it is important that you and your partner have a system of monitoring her most fertile times; which will allow you to have sex in her most fertile phase. To do this, you'll need a layman's understanding of the female reproductive cycle. This will allow you to calculate the times when pregnancy is most likely to occur, and then plan to have sex on those days.

Know Your Partner's Reproductive Cycle

Put this in the category of 'everything you ever wanted to know but were too afraid to ask'! If you're aiming to have sex in your partner's most fertile times you must be at one with the journey of the egg. At the end of this you'll both be able to develop a romantic timetable of intimate moments, increasing your chances of getting pregnant. Thankfully, some clever people have

Come On Aussie, Come On!

With all this sex-for-conception stuff happening at the moment, you have to be wondering how your efforts are contributing to Team Australia. Thankfully, the international condom manufacturer Durex has the answers.

Durex's 2005 sex survey included a staggering 317 000 participants from 41 countries. As an added bonus, almost all cricket- and rugby-playing nations were involved.

Greece (not famous for cricket) leads the world in sexual frequency at 138 times a year, trouncing the world average of 103 times a year (must be the climate). Australia comes sixteenth, with 108 times a year, narrowly beaten by South Africa on 109. For the record, Japan comes last, with 45 times a year.

In an amazing come-back, Australia comes in second internationally to Turkey in number of sexual partners, with Australia at 13.3 and Turkey at 14.5. Our Kiwi cousins come third with 13.2, while India comes in last at 3.3 – similar to the cricket, really.

In the age-of-first-sex stakes, Aussies averaged 16.8 years old. Iceland had the youngest average, at 15.6 years (climate again), and India the oldest at 19.8 years.

A plethora of other sexual facts about Australians and their sexual habits were also exposed in the survey. Seventy-three per cent had had sex in a car, 44 per cent wished they had sex more frequently, and last but not least, 44 per cent claimed to be happy with their sex life.

lavor Georgeff

divided the female cycle into main stages to help you. Here's the abridged version:

1. The Period: Days 1 to 5 (Menstruation)

The whole female reproductive thing, rather strangely, begins with the end of the previous month's cycle. (Why it's calculated this way is perhaps just to make the matter confusing.) At any rate, the reason for a period is that fertilisation hasn't taken place in the previous cycle, meaning the show's over and the lining of the uterus has fallen away. The duration of bleeding is variable but usually lasts around five days.

2. The Preparation: Days 5 to 13 (Follicular Phase)

This is the preparation part of the cycle, where the lining of the woman's womb begins to thicken and bulk up, and the egg gets ready to be released from little hair-like things called follicles.

3. Egg on the Move: Days 13 to 16 (Ovulation)

Somewhere from day 13 to 16, the follicles burst and the egg is released and starts its journey down the fallopian tube. If the ovum manages to hook up with the sperm in this time, then it's game on. Unfortunately, the egg has a short shelf life and will self-destruct in 24 hours if it doesn't get fertilised.

4. The Wait: Days 16 to 28 (Luteal Phase)

The womb waits for a hormonal calling card to confirm fertilisation. It will wait until day 28, and then, if pregnancy has not occurred, the cycle ends (or in actual fact, starts again).

Develop a Luuurve Calendar

So now that you've got a basic understanding of what's going on, let's look at the methods you and your partner can use to try and predict her most fertile time.

As the name indicates, a calendar-based method uses a calendar to chart your partner's approximate menstrual cycle in an attempt to try and predict her most fertile time. By setting a standard number of days based on the history of a woman's past cycle lengths, the technique tries to predict when a woman may be most fertile.

To do this, your partner's reproductive cycle must be pencilled onto a calendar. If her cycle is as regular as clockwork (a 28-day cycle is average, but cycles can vary from 20 to 45 days), by all means pencil in the dates her period is due over the course of the entire year. But if her cycle is less regular, take a punt on the average length of a cycle (it's helpful if your partner has kept a record for several months prior to her attempt to get pregnant of her cycle length: count the days between periods, average them, then use this figure to estimate the likely due date of her next and subsequent periods). It's a good idea to pencil in her menstrual due date month by month to avoid having to erase and re-pencil in a whole year's worth of details, in the event that one period comes a little earlier or later than usual.

Now, it's one thing for you and your partner to attempt to predict the average length of her cycle but predicting ovulation, and therefore the best time to have sex, is a little more complicated (unfortunately, ovulation doesn't occur smack-bang in the middle of her cycle). Many excellent websites provide this information – just type in 'ovulation calculator', choose a site and follow the leads. You will need to type in the date of the first day of your partner's last period, and how long her cycle usually lasts. Some websites need more complex information, like an exact ovulation date so it may be worthwhile investigating some of the system-based methods mentioned later in this chapter.

To get you started on your research, here is an example of a love calendar based on a 28-day cycle where ovulation is guesstimated over a four-day window period (in this case 13 to 16 April). Since sperm can live for approximately four days (while inside your

For once you must try not to shirk the facts: mankind is kept alive by bestial acts.
Bertolt Brecht

partner) regular sex from 10 through to 20 April will give you the best chance of pregnancy. Got it?

1 April Start of period	2	3	4	5 The preparation begins	6	7
8	9	10 Sex	11 Sex	12 Sex	13 Egg on the move Sex	14 Egg on the move Sex
15 Egg on the move Sex	16 Egg on the move Sex	17 The Wait ... Sex	18 Sex	19 Sex	20	21
22	23	24	25	26	27	28
29 Start of period. Try again!	30	1 May	2	3 The preparation begins!	4	5

Symptom-based Methods

OK, you've got the basic idea of the calendar thingy, but to throw a spanner into the works, the calendar provides approximate dates only, and unfortunately ovulation can potentially occur on two or three different days. So to help pinpoint the big day you can use symptom-based methods.

There are three basic symptoms, two of which are commonly charted to try and predict times of fertility.

Basal Body Temperature (BBT) is the lowest temperature of the body while resting. In practical terms, it is your partner's temperature when she first wakes up in the morning, before she gets up.

By taking her temperature each morning (you need a very sensitive thermometer) you can try to predict ovulation, as the hormones which start the fertile part of the cycle also cause a rise in body temperature. By charting this information you can then detect the spike in temperature, which can help both of you work out the best time to 'get it on'. Presumably this method is very popular with meteorologists.

Cervical mucus is another observable symptom which can be charted to try and predict your partner's most fertile times. Not that you have ever really wanted to know this, but cervical mucus is normally light and slightly sticky. In times leading up to fertility, however, it becomes clearer and less sticky, with an 'eggy' consistency. This consistency can be tested between the thumb and forefinger, hopefully without you actually having to see it. Presumably this approach is very popular with chefs.

The position of the cervix can also be used to try to predict fertility. In non-fertile times it tends to sit low in the vaginal canal and is firmer. In times leading up to fertility, however, the cervix rises higher in the vaginal canal and becomes softer. This is a less commonly used symptom-based method for predicting ovulation, as it can be a bit tricky for the layman (or woman) to detect the changes. But by all means try it out – one or both of you might even enjoy it! Presumably this method is very popular with, umm … cervix inspectors.

Other Methods
Ovulation predictor kits (OPKs) are available from pharmacies and work by detecting surges in hormones that trigger the release of a woman's eggs. Not the most romantic thing in the world, but heck, when the time is right then it's right for love!

These methods, all good on their own, can be put together on one sensational 'luuurve calendar' to help fine-tune and pinpoint the best days of the month on which to 'go for it' and, hopefully, maximise your chances of getting pregnant.

3. The Seek-Medical-Advice Approach
Been at it like rabbits but still no pregnancy? If so, it is important to get a doctor to see if there isn't another issue at play. The reasoning behind this is that if there are any problems, it's better to tackle them as soon as possible, as time often becomes a problem

when trying to treat fertility issues. If you or your partner can tick a box for any of the below issues, then don't try for a year before seeing a doctor; see one now.

In women, a history of any of the following may interfere with having a baby:
- any disease that might have caused scarring in the womb, like endometriosis, pelvic inflammatory disease or a previous sexually transmitted infection;
- diseases like Polycystic Ovarian Syndrome that prevent the release of the egg;
- irregular or painful periods;
- previous ectopic pregnancy, or miscarriages;
- a chronic disease like diabetes, cancer, thyroid disease, asthma or lupus;
- any chromosomal problems;
- taking medications that might interfere with pregnancy;
- smoking tobacco or marijuana;
- being overweight or underweight (men: if you are going to bring this to your partner's attention, do so with great diplomacy and tact!).

In men, a history of any of the following may interfere with having a baby:
- any chronic illness like diabetes, cancer or thyroid disease;
- a sexually transmitted disease, such as chlamydia or gonorrhoea;
- an infection with the mumps virus after puberty;
- any previous problems with the testicles (injury, cysts, tumours), or testicles that haven't moved into the scrotum;
- problems getting or maintaining an erection;
- problems ejaculating;
- any chromosomal problems;
- taking medications that might interfere with pregnancy;
- smoking tobacco or marijuana;
- working in a hot environment, or hobbies (such as using a hot tub) that could result in your testicles overheating;
- working with chemicals or radiation;
- being overweight.

If you do see a doctor, you may end up being sent for a barrage of tests in the attempt to establish exactly what is going on. Subsequent to being poked, prodded and asked many awkward questions regarding your sex life, you may be referred on to a fertility specialist.

Health Insurance

If you're not going down the public health path then you need to get private health insurance sorted out asap. Following are some questions and answers to some of the most significant issues concerning private health.

Q: *How long is the waiting period before you can use it?*

A: The government sets the maximum time that health insurers are able to make members wait until they can claim benefits for hospital treatment. For pregnancy, this maximum wait is 12 months. So if you and your partner think you'll need cover for pregnancy, you need to get the appropriate cover well before you get pregnant.

Q: *Does the policy include obstetrics?*

A: Many cheaper policies do not include obstetrics, or pay restricted benefits that may only cover obstetrics as a private patient attending a public hospital. If you want the birth to be in a private hospital with obstetrics, you need to seek out the appropriate policy. Also check whether an emergency caesarean section is included.

Q: *Does the policy include costs throughout pregnancy, birth and after the baby is born?*

A: If you have a single membership and you want the child to be covered at birth, it needs to be transferred to family membership or a single-parent family membership in order to cover the newborn. Remember to check with the insurer to see how soon this needs to be done – it is usually required several months before the child is born.

Q: *What about life insurance?*

A: It's probably as good a time as any to have a think about life insurance for both working and stay-at-home parents. This way, in the event that if anything were to happen to you or your partner, your child and family would be taken care of financially.

Improving Your Health

Whatever way you're trying to conceive, if you want to give yourselves the best chance at procreation it's important that you and your partner are physically fit.

Look guys, some health issues (like genetic disease) are serious and do affect your chances to conceive and go through to have a healthy child. But most of us who may not be at the peak of fitness can still go on to have a beautiful healthy bub. So why bother getting buffed? It improves your chances of conception and since you're going to be doing a whole lot of loving ... it may well improve your stamina too.

Body Weight

Studies have shown that excess body weight may affect fertility in both males and females. It is thought that too much or too little body weight may play a part in disrupting reproductive hormones and, in turn, the ability to produce healthy sperm or ova.

Both men and women with a body mass index of more than 29 are likely to be less fertile and take longer than average to conceive, while women with a body mass index of less than 19 are more likely to be less fertile. In short, having a healthy body weight in both sexes will increase the likelihood of fertility.

Diet

Ever wondered why Ronald McDonald doesn't have kids? You are what you eat, and a healthy diet has a direct relation to the health of your sperm. In women, diet is particularly important for trying to conceive and it is thought that an unbalanced diet may contribute to the body weight conception issues mentioned above. Vitamin B is one vitamin that has been shown to improve the chance of maintaining a normal pregnancy. In most foods it is known as folate and is found in dark green vegetables, fruit and fruit juice, potatoes (in their jackets), beans and Vegemite.

Stress

Some research suggests that stress, apart from handicapping you and your partner in the Bedroom Olympics might affect certain hormones that are needed for conception.

Alligators, Polar Bears and Yours Truly

All is not well in the world, with alligators in Florida being found with reduced penis size, polar bears discovered with both male and female genitals, and strong scientific evidence being recorded of dramatic drops in human sperm count.

The main culprits for these alarming trends appear to be chemicals known as xeno-oestrogens. These chemicals, commonly used in pesticides, drugs and other industrial chemicals, mimic the female hormone oestrogen and affect animal reproductive systems.

In the case of Florida's alligators, one lake system in which they live had been heavily polluted with the insecticide DDT in the 1980s. The alligators themselves showed extremely low levels of testosterone, coupled with abnormal testicular development. Furthermore, their penises were roughly half the size of normal alligators.

Hermaphrodite polar bears are suspected of ingesting large amounts of chemicals because of their position at the top of the food chain. (Larger animals eat smaller animals, which in turn eat smaller animals, and so on, and harmful chemicals build up in ever-increasing density in the fatty tissues.) Bad luck for the unsuspecting polar bears.

Although the jury is still out on the cause, a seminal (no pun intended) study published in 1992 by the Dane Dr Skakkebaek acted as a house of cards in the worldwide realisation that sperm counts were going the way of the dinosaur.

Skakkebaek's team reviewed the literature on 61 worldwide studies going back to 1938 and concluded that there was a clear trend in declining sperm counts, with averaged sperm counts plummeting from 113 million in 1940 to 66 million in 1990. In a nutshell, mankind's nuts weren't quite right.

Since Dr Skakkebaek's study, a multitude of other studies have clearly demonstrated dropping sperm counts in certain countries or regions – an alarming observation which seems to suggest that environmental influences are at work. Lower counts can be strongly correlated with an area's production of synthetic chemicals (agricultural pesticides appear to be a major culprit), the number of automobiles in a region, and a community's overall consumption of meat, fat and alcohol.

Reasons for the depressing phenomenon are various, but one thing is clear: the modern sperm has a lot to deal with.

Drugs

All the stuff we take that affects our bodies are drugs. This includes antibiotics and other things prescribed by doctors, socially 'accepted' things like alcohol and tobacco and illegal recreational substances. Some of these drugs, legal or otherwise can affect your partner's chance to conceive, maintain a pregnancy and give birth to a healthy baby.

Lay Off the Booze

A large percentage of the population uses alcohol as a social lubricant – and, let's face it, many a coupling couple may never have met if it weren't for a few bevies. Despite this, it is probably best for both males and females to limit alcohol intake when trying to get pregnant. High alcohol intake is known to damage sperm and to cause a number of nasty problems in women, including decreased fertility and menstrual disorders.

Quit Smoking

It's no surprise that something that is proven to kill people is going to affect your fertility. Studies have shown smokers to be up to half as fertile as non-smokers, and it has been proven that smoking negatively affects sperm morphology and motility.

For women, smoking can cause early menopause and menstrual problems. Evidence also shows that smoking during pregnancy can increase the risk of miscarriage, premature delivery, stillbirth and low-birth-weight babies. Other evidence also suggests that smoking while pregnant can pass cancer-causing agents on to the foetus.

What more do you need to know? Give the fags a miss!

Ask About Prescription Drugs

If you are taking prescription drugs, and this advice should be followed for over-the-counter purchases as well, it is important to ask about their possible effects on your fertility, as there are many prescription (and over-the-counter) drugs which may inhibit your ability to conceive.

Steroid Use

Probably only relevant to the severe gym junkies among us, the use of steroids, which are usually taken illegally, can (rather ironically) shrink your testicles and reduce sperm production.

Avoid Recreational Drug Use
Yup, you guessed it, along with tobacco, booze and steroids, recreational drugs are also not going to help your sperm be at the top of their game. Marijuana is known to affect sperm motility, while other recreational drugs, such as cocaine and ecstasy, have been shown to reduce sperm count and affect the shape and function of your little wrigglers.

Your Partner and Recreational Drugs
Recreational drugs also affect your partner's ability to conceive and maintain a healthy pregnancy. Drug use has been linked with absent or irregular periods (probably through weight loss), while more specifically cannabis has been linked with birth defects and cocaine has been linked to miscarriage.

Occupational Hazards
As if the nine-to-five grind isn't bad enough, it may also be affecting your fertility. Some occupations may involve exposure to hazards (chemicals, radiation, excessive heat) that can affect both male and female fertility. People who are concerned about this should seek the appropriate advice from their doctor.

Tackle Tips (For Men Only)
The healthiness of sperm, and therefore the chances of conception, is judged by a number of criteria, including volume, concentration, motility (movement) and morphology (shape). Further to this, the presence of too many white blood cells in semen can impact on the health and wellbeing of your sperm.

Factors that may affect sperm count include environmental toxins, genetic problems and age. If you are concerned that your sperm count may be low, see your family doctor. In the meantime there are a number of things you can do to ensure your sperm is as healthy as it can be for the big swim ahead.

Flu Warning!
Although it's out of your control, it's worth noting that a viral infection such as the flu can knock your sperm around for up to three months. This is because the sperm being made at the time of an influenza or other viral infection will take about 90 days to fully mature and come off the production line. Although a flu

Healthy Sperm as Defined by WHO (World Health Organization)

The World Health Organization provides the following definition of a 'normal' sperm count:

- The concentration of spermatozoa should be at least 20 million per millilitre;
- The total volume of semen should be at least 2 ml;
- The total number of spermatozoa in the ejaculate should be at least 40 million;
- At least 75 per cent of the spermatozoa should be alive (it is normal for up to 25 per cent to be dead);
- At least 30 per cent of the spermatozoa should be of normal shape and form;
- At least 25 per cent of the spermatozoa should be swimming with rapid forward movement;
- At least 50 per cent of the spermatozoa should be swimming forward, even if only sluggishly.

probably won't knock them into infertility if they (and you) are already in shape, the thinking goes that if a man has borderline fertility, a virus may push his fertility over the edge for a period of time.

Get Into Free-balling

Those tight-jean-clad eighties rock-gods never knew what they were doing to themselves. Tight or synthetic pants or underwear may inhibit sperm production by pulling the scrotum closer to the body and increasing the temperature of the testes. It is thought that the testes hang free to provide sperm with an optimum temperature, so increasing this temperature ain't a good thing. So, shelve the grandpa Y-fronts and skin-tight denims of your youth and hang loose: cotton boxers and chinos are sperm-friendly and positively de rigueur.

Avoid Excessive Ejaculation and Prolonged Abstinence

Both are known to affect the number and quality of sperm. Intercourse every two to three days at prime fertility times is thought to maintain sperm quality.

Supplements

Folic acid intake in combination with zinc sulphate has been shown to have often dramatic effects on sperm counts. Some men, when taking these supplements, increased their sperm count by as much as 74 per cent.

Techniques for Improving Conception

Apart from actually having sex, there are a number of well-accepted (but as yet unproven) tips to increase the chances of pregnancy during and after sex.

Position, Position, Position!

Although no definitive studies have been done on sexual positions increasing chances of pregnancy, the missionary position is widely regarded as an ideal position to enhance the chances of getting

Folic Acid and Zinc Sulphate May Increase Sperm Count

A 2002 study conducted at the Nijmegan University Medical Centre in the Netherlands demonstrated the promising effects of combined folic acid and zinc sulphate supplements on sperm count. The study followed the effects of the supplements on sperm quality in 108 fertile men and 103 infertile men over 26 weeks. Individual members of both groups were assigned one of four treatments: (1) zinc alone (15 mg per day), (2) folic acid alone (5 mg per day), (3) zinc plus folic acid, or (4) a placebo.

Before and after assessments of sperm concentration, motility and morphology were made in accordance with the World Health Organization's guidelines, with blood levels of zinc and folate also measured.

The sub-fertile group showed a significant increase in sperm quality after combined zinc sulphate and folic acid treatment, with a 74 per cent increase. There was also a 4 per cent improvement in abnormal spermatozoa. The fertile group of men followed a similar trend.

Although the beneficial effects of the study on infertility are yet to be established, the results show promising prospects for future infertility treatments.

pregnant. This is because it allows for the deepest penetration, ensuring that sperm are deposited close to the cervix. It is also thought preferable to avoid positions where the woman is on top, which may give cause for the little fellas to fight against gravity, therefore hindering the flow of semen to the egg.

Where's the Egg, Dudes?

A study by scientists at the State University of New York at Buffalo sheds some light on the effects of tetrahydrocannabinol (THC), the active ingredient in cannabis, on the swimming ability of sperm. The research compared the sperm of 22 'frequent' cannabis smokers and 59 non-cannabis-smoking men. 'Frequent' in this case meant that the subjects smoked an average of 14 times a week over five years. (Pass the jar, man.)

The study's conclusion showed that the cannabis smokers produced less sperm and seminal fluid than their non-smoking compatriots, and that their sperm were more likely to swim too fast too early. The relevance of the study to those who smoke cannabis is this: a regular dope smoker with an already-low sperm count may be in danger of being pushed over the edge into infertility.

A further study reported in New Scientist involved test tubes of sperm being treated with THC. The sperm (much like dope smokers themselves) meandered lazily, without any sense of direction. Those sperm that did manage to find the egg were unable to bind with it or penetrate it. In surprising contrast to the effects of THC on sperm, Brazilian researchers from Sao Paolo University have shown that coffee may have a positive effect on sperm. The researchers divided 750 men into four groups. The groups were established by how many 100 ml cups of coffee a day each man drank, and were divided into: (1) non-coffee drinkers, (2) one- to three-cup-a-dayers, (3) four- to six-cup-a-dayers, and (4) more-than-six-cup-a-dayers. Of the four groups, it was discovered that all three coffee-drinking groups had higher sperm motility than the non-coffee-drinking group. This led the researchers to the conclusion that certain compounds in coffee may aid in infertility problems in the future.

Funding your local café's staff holiday, or spending your waking hours in a super-charged state, may be a bit premature, however, as researchers have not yet concluded whether caffeine-induced motility in sperm actually improves their fertility.

Relax Afterwards (Not You!)

If your partner is the sort of person who likes a game of tennis or a quick run straight after sex, it's time to tell her to slow things down a bit.

To improve chances of conception, the laws of gravity suggest that your partner should lie on her back with her hips slightly raised after intercourse. She should remain in this pose for at least 15 minutes. The thinking is that this position will allow the sperm time to get to where they want to go with minimum fuss.

Sex is the most fun you can have without laughing.

Woody Allen

Have Good Sex

The clock is ticking, the time is right, hurry up, we're making a baby this time … ! It is important to try and have enjoyable sex while trying to conceive, and keep up the romance, mainly because it takes the pressure off both parties involved.

Spiky Love

If you think your partner can sometimes be a bit prickly in response to your sexual desires, spare a thought for the poor male echidna.

His mating ritual involves following the female in a 'train' of two to eight possible suitors for up to a week. When the female gets in the mood and finally finds a tree she likes, she fastens herself to it with her front legs. This show of unadulterated sexuality prompts the love-struck males to dig a circular trench around the tree, about 25 centimetres in depth.

Then, as if the whole foreplay thing wasn't arduous enough, the males wrestle in order to evict one another from the trench.

Once one lucky wrestler is left, the champion then gets the chance to do the business by lying on his back and carefully positioning himself under the female in order to avoid those sharp spikes. Ouch!

www.commons.wikimedia.org/Allan Whittome

Size Matters

The world of mammalian penis size is enough to make any man a tad insecure. First there's the blue whale with his 5-metre-long member, then there's the 80 centimetre erection of the stallion, dwarfing the average man's 15 centimetre erection. Take heart, however, as among primates the human male's penis comes in on top ... so to speak. (Gorillas measure 3 centimetres erect, orangutans nearly 4 centimetres and chimps about 13 centimetres.)

www.commons.wikimedia.org

But testicles are another matter. The combined weight of a man's testes averages 42 grams – slightly higher than those nightclub bouncers of the jungle, gorillas, yet minuscule when compared to the 113 gram testes of a 45 kilogram male chimp.

The reason for variation in testes size is frequency of copulation – and, therefore, amount of sperm needed to do the job. The poor gorilla only manages to do the business a couple of times a year, and then only for about a minute, which seems to shed light on all that frustrated chest-beating. At the other end of the scale, the highly promiscuous chimp has sex on tap with his harem, with daily opportunities to copulate with multiple partners – what a tart! Man copulates more than gorillas and less than chimps, putting their testes size somewhere in between.

Although there is no solid anthropological explanation for the length of man's oversized endowment, as compared to his primate cousins, it is suspected that size may act in the way peacock feathers do – to attract females.

The question unanswered in all this is, who goes around measuring the erect penises of gorillas, and how the hell do they do it?

Time of Day

Rise and shine, and stay in bed. Studies have shown that sperm counts are higher earlier in the day. So trying to fertilise your partner's eggs before you have your own sunny-side-up may slightly increase chances of conception.

The Signs of Pregnancy

So, Big Boy, you've cleaned up your act, got healthy and sown the seeds on demand at the right time without pausing to give a thought for yourself. Phew, that was hard work! But have you found fertile soil? The following signs should indicate whether or not all that back-breaking toil was worth it.

No Period. Period.

The first sign that there may be a bun in the oven is a late menstrual period. Don't celebrate too early, however: the period must be at least two weeks late from the date it's expected to be a reliable sign of pregnancy.

Shagged

Fatigue is a sign of pregnancy, as your partner's body is more biologically active than usual in its pregnant state. Progesterone is produced in a higher volume, depressing the central nervous system and causing drowsiness. Additionally, the volume and flow of blood increases in order to service the growing placenta. All this blood pumping means the heart is working harder, which can also contribute to lethargy.

No matter how much cats fight, there always seem to be plenty of kittens.

Abraham Lincoln

Morning Sickness

Thousands, if not millions, of pregnant women will show their contempt for the 'morning' part of this term by retching on you at any time of the day. Rising hormone levels and a heightened sense of smell cause nausea and vomiting in approximately 50 per cent of pregnancies, typically at any time of day, including the morning.

Pregnancy 101

OK, tiger, admit it, you know nothing about pregnancy and how it all works. Well, read this and you will. There are three parts to the whole pregnancy thing:

1. Pregnancy

A normal pregnancy lasts from 37 to 42 weeks. But for convenience a pregnancy is considered to be 40 weeks duration. It is divided into three trimesters, or three parts.

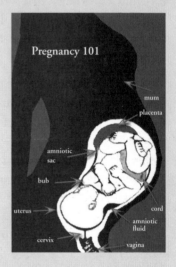

2. Labour and Birth

Labour is the process of evicting a baby from its home in the uterus. This is done through the tightening of the muscle in the womb (called a contraction) and by active pushing from your partner. It is also divided into three parts:

1st stage – the cervix opens
2nd stage – the baby is pushed out
3rd stage – the placenta is expelled from the womb.
Note: The above process is not for the faint-hearted!

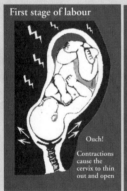

First stage of labour

Ouch!
Contractions cause the cervix to thin out and open

Second stage of labour

Baby escapes through the fully opened cervix! They are forced out through contractions and pushing!

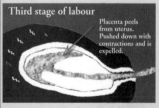

Third stage of labour

Placenta peels from uterus. Pushed down with contractions and is expelled.

3. After the Baby is Born

This part of pregnancy involves getting the baby sorted and returning your partner's body back to its pre-pregnancy state, ready for round two!

Light Vaginal Bleeding

You may be lucky enough (not!) to notice a light vaginal bleeding or a slight brown vaginal discharge from your partner. Light blood loss early in pregnancy, usually on day six or seven, can indicate implantation of the placenta into the wall of the uterus. However, bleeding is not always a sign of a successful pregnancy. If your partner has a lot of vaginal bleeding (more than her normal menstrual flow), she should get it checked out by a health professional.

Breast Enlargement (God Must Be a Man!)

One of the added bonuses of selflessly dealing with vomiting, mood swings, unexpected bleeding and fatigue in your poor, suffering partner is an increase in breast size. Not yours, by the way.

A woman's breasts enlarge as early as two weeks into pregnancy to prepare for milk production. Lemons miraculously ripen into melons, melons into sublime erotic fruit. Ridiculously expensive push-up bras hibernate in unused drawers, and all is good in the world. However, be aware that her breasts are probably tender, and what with this, her nausea, fatigue, etc., there is probably a slim chance of you getting anywhere near them!

Pregnancy Testing

The best thing to do if you think your partner may have a bun in the oven is to pop down to the pharmacist's and get a pregnancy test kit. If the result is positive, your partner should get to a doctor to have the results confirmed with a blood test. If all is well, your doctor will probably also organise some of the other testing she will need in early pregnancy.

Movin' On ...

OK, so all of this sex-for-pregnancy stuff was more complex than you thought. Well, it's not, really. Just put this book down and turn off the light, Big Boy ...

If All Else Fails, Remember:

- Sex is a bit like pizza: even when it's bad it's good.
- It's a bit like learning to ride a bicycle: if you fall off you have to get straight back on again and keep on trying until you get it right.
- When you are eventually successful in your endeavours you're unlikely to be getting much for a while, so make the most of it while you can!

Useful Contacts

Access National Infertility Network (AUS)
www.access.org.au
Tel: 02 9637 0158
Information about infertility, links and support.

Alcohol and Drug Information Service (AUS)
www.adin.com.au
The Australian Drug Information Network
Tel: 1800 888 236
This government service provides alcohol and drug information and contact information.

Andrology Australia (AUS)
www.andrologyaustralia.org
Tel: 1300 303 878
Information on specific areas of male reproductive health.

Family Planning
(ACT) www.shfpact.org.au; tel: 02 6247 3077
(NSW) www.fpansw.org.au; tel: 02 8252 4300
(NT) www.fpwnt.com.au; 08 8948 0144
(QLD) www.fpq.com.au; tel: 07 3250 0240
(SA) www.shinesa.org.au; tel: 08 8300 5300
(TAS) www.fpt.asn.au; tel: 03 6228 5244
(VIC) www.fpv.org.au; tel: 03 9257 0100
(WA) www.fpwa.org.au; tel: 08 9227 6177
State links to family planning, contraception, pregnancy and youth sites.

Endometriosis Association of Victoria (VIC)
www.endometriosis.org.au
Tel: 03 9562 7555
Providing support for women with endometriosis.

Fertility Society of Australia (AUS)
www.fertilitysociety.com.au
Tel: 03 9645 6359
Representing scientists, doctors, researchers, nurses, consumer groups, patients and counsellors in reproductive medicine in Australia and New Zealand.

Nutrition Australia (AUS)
www.nutritionaustralia.org
Tel: 03 9650 5165
Offers web-based information about healthy eating.

Polycystic Ovarian Syndrome Association of Australia (AUS)
www.posaa.asn.au
Tel: 02 8250 0222
A support and advocacy group for women and teenagers with Polycystic Ovarian Syndrome.

Quit (AUS)
www.quitnow.info.au
Tel: 13 18 48
The facts on smoking, plus advice and support on quitting.

Relationships Australia (AUS)
www.relationships.com.au
Tel: 1300 364 277
Resources for couples, individuals and families to enhance and support relationships.

Sexual Health and Family Planning Australia
www.shfpa.org.au
Tel: 02 6198 3415
A national federation of eight independent state and territory sexual health and family planning organisations.

2

Dazed and Confused

How Are You Going To Do This? Checklist

☑ Get over your swagger and/or shock – there are important decisions to be made here!

☑ Do a little research: find out what options for obstetric care are available in your area.

☑ Sit down over a refreshing cup of low-caffeine herbal tea and choose a caregiver.

☑ If you've decided on private healthcare, get insurance *now*.

☑ Finish off all outstanding hobbies and DIY projects in the next week: The birdhouse, the home-shaped surfboard, the million-dollar bottle-opener-in-a-bottle idea, that abstract painting thing you started five years ago, and the string theory rebuttal thesis you've been thinking about. You're going to be very short of time very soon.

☑ Arrange a wake with that larrikin single mate your partner thinks is a bad influence, buy him some flowers or something, you're going to be in a different orbit pretty soon.

☑ Arrange to get to the pub/footy/nightclub with some hairy mates … Oh yes … it's going to be a long time between drinks for you buddy!

The test is back and it's positive. If it wasn't planned you're probably in some state of deep, almost comatose, shock. Alternatively, if it was planned, you're probably in some state of deep, almost comatose, shock.

Being a male, after a few days the shock will subside and you'll start to get a bit of a macho swagger. That sort of 'Hey, I better walk like a cowboy 'cause there's a lot going on downstairs' sort of thing.

Much to the alarm of all concerned, you'll high-five the local shop owner, your monster mother-in-law, your arch-bastard work associates and possibly even your own partner. This is all because you have, and let's be clear about this, single-handedly proven Darwin's theory of natural selection. Furthermore, You, with a capital Y, are now irreplaceable in the workings of the world.

Unfortunately the swagger will quickly turn into an insecure limp as reality starts to sink in. Insert appropriate expletives in the questions you've been asking yourself below.

'_____!, a kid, *I'm* still a kid, aren't I?!'

'_____!, a kid, that's actually quite a lot of responsibility, isn't it?!'

'_____!, a kid, I better get my shit together?!'

You may also, quite stupidly, be in a state of denial:

'_____!, a kid, it won't change my life that much, I'll still be able to do all those things I do now, won't I?'

If these thoughts are grating on your everyday life, sit back, breathe deeply and let go, as the sooner you come to terms with it the easier it's going to be. Yes, it's a lot of responsibility and it's going to demand some pretty drastic life changes, but at the end of the day the whole experience ahead of you is going to be infinitely more positive than negative, as anybody who's gone through it will tell you.

Think about it, your parents had kids and you're OK, aren't you?

So, now that we have that over and done with, and you're still in a state of panic, let's think about what's ahead. On the positive side, nine months, beyond the biological demands of pregnancy, is actually a good amount of time for you and your partner to get your heads around what you've got yourselves into.

Imagine if your wife casually cocked her leg and jettisoned a fully jump-suited individual who swore at you before slinking off in the direction of the closest shopping mall. In this scenario, a couple of weeks of pregnancy would probably be enough preparation, but it's not going to happen.

You have just entered the first trimester, the first three months of your partner's pregnancy. Gestation – the period from conception to delivery – will be approximately 266 days (count 'em), or roughly nine months.

So, what to tackle first?

On the practical side you're going to have to make some fairly important decisions about what obstetric care your partner and future child receive in this pregnancy. In Australia today there is a bewildering range of ways to have a baby, and the odds are you will know nothing about what's on offer, so read this chapter and school-up. Knowledge is power.

Caregivers: Who's Who in the Zoo?

Let's get to know some of the players in pregnancy care, as it will help you understand what they can provide for your partner and baby. Basically, anyone who looks after your partner is a caregiver, and there are two different types of caregivers in pregnancy: midwives and obstetricians. Generally speaking, midwives and obstetricians work together and you will be meeting them both at some stage of the pregnancy.

Midwives

Midwives are professionals qualified to look after your partner throughout their whole pregnancy, which includes before, during and after the birth. Midwives may work independently or as part of a team with obstetricians.

Midwives are trained through university in a three-year degree, with a year of on-the-job training, before they are qualified. When they work without an

Male midwives are called midwives as well, not 'midhusbands' as you might expect.

www.commons.wikimedia.org

Lions, Pregnancy and Your Role as a Health Consumer

In the good old days, men were expected to defend the women and children of the tribe from marauding lions and other hostile forces. Today we have it easy and have lost our mojo. Women are empowered and children are virtually brought up by Xbox, so our traditional role of 'protectors of the weak' has been seriously curtailed.

Now that your partner is pregnant, however, you can once more step up to the plate and shine. By having an understanding of pregnancy, childbirth and some issues involved you can advocate (that means support and defend – we looked it up too) for your partner and child, ensuring they receive spot-on care.

If you've previously been fit and healthy, having a baby might well be your first foray into the complicated world of healthcare. Whatever way you choose to have your baby, your caregivers (midwives, doctors and others) will know more about pregnancy than you. So, as to what's going on and what to expect, it is important to be an informed and responsible healthcare consumer. Be sure to:

- Do your homework: read up and ask lots of questions.
- Be active with your partner in making decisions. If your caregiver suggests a line of treatment you don't understand, ask them to explain until you and your partner are both comfortable.
- Know your partner's rights while in hospital (see 'Know Your Rights and Responsibilities, Brother', page 42).

An obstetrician preparing to deliver a baby.

obstetrician they specialise in normal pregnancy, birth and post-natal care. They can be male or female (males are called midwives as well, not 'midhusbands', as you might expect).

Obstetricians

An obstetrician is a doctor who has specialist training in maternity care (called obstetrics). He or she attends medical school and then undertakes extensive hospital and obstetric college training before becoming qualified. Obstetricians lead teams of doctors and work with midwives, who collectively provide care for your partner and baby.

Other Players

Other caregivers may have a role in looking after your partner and baby. They include:

Midwives, Bonfires and the Grand Inquisition

Modern midwives are well-respected professionals. However, travel back to the Middle Ages and midwives, rather unfairly, had a darker reputation. 'The better the witch, the better the midwife' was a popular medieval saying.

The folk ideology of the time imagined a link between midwives and the supernatural, and sadly, this was a belief that would see many midwives sent to the flames (and we're not talking head-wetting barbecues). The fearsome Grand Inquisition, after burning all the harmless heretics and social odd-bods in Europe, became obsessed with witches and witchcraft. Accusations of witchcraft fell on older women, eccentrics and practitioners of folk medicine and midwifery.

Sadly, not much evidence was needed to bring a person to trial for witchcraft. Before the Grand Inquisition, hearsay and slander could see the innocent burned alive. Historian and novelist Jonathan Kirsch brings one such story to life. In the picturesque Alps, a Swiss midwife call Dichtlin was accused of witchcraft in 1502. The son of a rival midwife brought the matter before the Inquisition, claiming Dichtlin was so overcome with a sense of professional rivalry that she had used sorcery to kill his mother. The son claimed his mother denounced Dichtlin with her dying breath. Although not something that would have excited Sherlock Holmes, to the presumed mortal disadvantage of Dichtlin the matter was actually brought to trial. Not content with having a go just at Dichtlin, her daughter was also accused of witchcraft (it was claimed that she started a violent downpour of rain by washing in a local creek). What happened to this hapless Swiss mother and daughter has not been recorded, but without the need for strong evidence to achieve a conviction, the outcome for Dichtlin and her daughter may not have been pretty.

Nurses

Nursing will be found in all speciality areas of a hospital where your partner or baby may need care. In the obstetric setting you may meet some nurses who are experts in mothercraft (baby handling), which includes stuff like feeding, bathing and child settling. They can be a fantastic resource to help you make the transition from hip young things to greying new parents.

Nurses are angels in comfortable shoes.

Author unknown

Doctors

You may meet doctors working under an obstetrician, or providing some kind of specialised care to your partner or baby. Doctors tend to thoughtfully write stuff on clipboards and are generally very clever people.

General Practitioners (GPs)

GPs can provide some of the care your partner will receive before she has the baby. However, they aren't involved in the birth or the period following the birth of your baby. Some GPs are also obstetricians – called, funnily enough, GP obstetricians. In regional and remote areas they often provide some of the services an obstetrician would provide in a city setting.

Anaesthetists

They provide the anaesthetic drugs that put you to sleep before an operation and look after you while the surgeon cuts and snips. They are generally the doctors you meet in preparation for a caesarean.

Therefore God dealt well with the midwives: and the people multiplied and waxed very mighty.

Old Testament

Care Throughout the Pregnancy

Now that we have cast some light on the caregivers, let's look at what needs to be done to help the baby grow, be born and get home. It's important to have a bit of background information in order to try and make sense of

Dr Ignaz Semmelweis, Saviour of Women

This is the tale of how one historical obstetric figure took on the medical establishment and paid a terrible price for the good of birth practices today.

Dr Ignaz Semmelweis is remembered by many as the saviour of women. This Hungarian obstetrician and all-round hell-man was a frontrunner in the search for a theory of disease. For this contribution he lost his career and became the subject of ridicule … all for the seemingly logical (in our view) suggestion that doctors wash their hands.

In Vienna during the 1840s, Semmelweis was working as a junior doctor in the maternity ward of a large hospital. He noticed that one particular birthing room was making women very sick. He made a point of trying to find out why.

This birthing room was like any other in the hospital, apart from one fact: it was staffed by medical students. Part of the students' study load was to learn about anatomy through autopsy, and Semmelweis noted that the medical students were coming straight from their autopsy lessons to assist in labour. He started to wonder whether anything could be on the hands of the students that might have been causing illness in the maternity patients.

Throwing social convention to the wind, he conducted an experiment. He ordered his doctors and medical students to wash their hands with a chlorinated solution before examining women in labour. The results were remarkable. Following the hand-washing regimen, the rate of infections in the maternity ward dropped to less than 1 per cent.

The passionate Semmelweis took his results to the medical establishment, but they were affronted by his radical ideas and responded with hostility. A terrible political battle followed. Semmelweis accused his critics of being 'murderers and ignoramuses', but despite his colourful language he lost the fight and resigned from the hospital, and from practising medicine.

Poor Dr Semmelweis's ideas were way ahead of his time – even at the time of his death the medical community still largely ridiculed his view. Today he is remembered as an obstetrician who sacrificed his career and gave his all for the women under his care.

www.commons.wikimedia.org

Politics and Childbirth 101

In Australia a vigorous debate rages about what is the safest approach to birth. Medical science has provided life-saving interventions like the caesarean, which is used frequently in this country. However, every silver lining has a cloud, and these interventions come with risks.

A movement exists, comprising midwives, mothers and other professionals, that aims to improve safety in birthing by reducing unnecessary interventions. While recognising the importance of appropriate treatment, these guys want to shift birthing away from interventions in hospital and back to more natural environments, such as the home.

Their claim that interventions are over-utilised is supported by World Health Organization (WHO) data published in 1999. Australia's rates of interventions in pregnancy were found to be higher than their (the WHO's) recommendations. For example, the Australian caesarean rate is over 20 per cent – more than double the 10 per cent rate as suggested by the WHO.

Members of the Commonwealth government became alarmed at these findings and sought to revolutionise the way maternity services were offered in Australia by launching the National Maternity Action Plan in 2002. In this plan a reduction of interventions was pushed, and the government proposed to allow midwives access to Medicare funding. This funding would have offered a greater access to birthing away from the hospital setting and consequently away from unnecessary interventions.

The Professional Obstetrician Group's reaction to the National Maternity Action Plan was

what services different caregivers offer. Care in the pregnancy can be divided into three sections.

1. Care During Pregnancy (Antenatal Care)

All the services caregivers provide to your pregnant partner before she goes into labour are called antenatal care. That's 'ante' as in before and 'natal' as in birth. You may ask, what's wrong with 'before-birth care'? Who knows; that's just the way it is! Antenatal care includes check-ups, scans and tests.

2. Care in Labour (Intrapartum Care)

This is the care that occurs during labour and birth (bet you're negative. They believed that the percentage of Australia's obstetric interventions was not only appropriate, but believed it helped to make Australia one of the safest places in the world to give birth. Instead of obstetric interventions being dangerous, their slant was that the practice of home birthing carried the most risk of serious complications.

The government then changed tack: interventions were no longer the focus; home birthing was now the target. The government made it compulsory for midwives to obtain indemnity insurance to home birth. However, this proved near impossible for practitioners, as the insurance was extremely costly. Requests for funding from the government were refused. Simultaneously, legislation was prepared to fine uninsured midwives $30 000 for participating in home births.

These moves effectively made home birthing illegal. Outraged by their infringement of rights, women and midwives rallied in the streets of Canberra, demanding the government withdraw what they believed to be an injustice.

The government then found themselves stuck between a rock and a hard place. The threat of the fine was dropped and midwives were permitted to attend home births while uninsured until 2012. It was decided that more evidence was required to determine what comprised safe practice. Data on the subject is currently being collected. In 2012, evidence will be examined and decisions will be made. It is thought that either insurance will become available to midwives, or home birthing will be incorporated into the public health system.

Watch this space.

looking forward to that!). It includes things like monitoring the wellbeing of your partner and baby in labour, helping her get through labour, and offering pain relief (to your parter – not you!)

3. Care After the Baby is Born (Postnatal Care)
This is the stuff that occurs after the baby is born and may include things like monitoring your partner and child's wellbeing following birth, offering support and education about feeding and general baby care, and providing the tests and immunisations that the baby needs before going home.

Services in Australia

Let's explore what services are available in Australia and briefly discuss what they offer in each stage of pregnancy. This wide brown land is a big place with a complicated healthcare system, so there are going to be some local variations in services available, but these are your basic options:

1. Private Midwife

You can choose a private midwife (called an independent midwife). These health professionals offer your partner care throughout her pregnancy in the comfort of her own living room (or, if she prefers, in a midwife's clinic). At the time of writing, midwives offer only home-birth services, though in the near future they may be able to offer birthing in public hospitals. All postnatal services offered by a private midwife take place in your partner's home.

Private midwives come from a philosophy that birth is a natural process that is at its safest without unnecessary interventions. Normally your partner will need to be in good health and have an uncomplicated obstetric and gynaecological history to use this option. Private midwives offer very personal service and try to accommodate your wishes if it is safe to do so (for example, a water birth). 'How would you like your placenta cooked, Madame?'

If you want a private midwife, expect to pay the full costs. Fees are not currently refundable under Medicare or private health insurance schemes.

2. Private Obstetrician in a Public or Private Hospital

You can choose a private obstetrician who will offer a full range of services in both public and

In nothing do men more nearly approach the gods than in giving health to men.

Cicero

Restore a man to his health, his purse lies open to thee

Robert Burton

private hospitals. Obstetricians are doctors who have had a lot of experience in maternity care. They provide personalised care during pregnancy but delegate a lot of the care to others during labour and following the birth. If you wish to go to a private hospital, you will need a private obstetrician.

Your partner will deliver in a labour ward, and she and the new bub will be cared for in a postnatal ward. Having delegated most of the care for your partner and child to midwives and other doctors, the private obstetrician will usually assess your partner before discharge from hospital.

The majority of the costs for a private obstetrician and private hospital fees are covered by health insurance schemes, but there are usually some out-of-pocket expenses.

3. Public Patient in a Public Hospital

As a citizen or resident of Australia, your partner can have free care in public hospitals under the Medicare scheme. Your partner will be assigned an obstetrician but in most cases will not meet this specialist. This is of no concern, as a team of midwives, doctors and others will carry out the actual care of your partner and baby.

As a public patient your partner will, in the course of her pregnancy, receive care at the antenatal clinic located in the public hospital in which she will give birth. Midwives provide care in the clinics, with intermittent assessments by an obstetrician. Generally, all the tests and scans your partner requires will be organised through the hospital.

During labour, a team of midwives will care for your partner and baby in the labour ward. If any medical problems arise, an obstetrician will

My obstetrician was so dumb that when I gave birth he forgot to cut the cord. For a year that kid followed me everywhere. It was like having a dog on a leash.

Joan Rivers

Know Your Rights and Responsibilities, Brother

Whether you are in the private or public setting, your partner and baby have certain rights and responsibilities while in hospital. These rights and responsibilities are enshrined in a range of state laws and have been put forward in a nationwide draft charter for patient rights. Generally as a patient you have the right to:

- be treated with reasonable care and skill by your caregivers;
- decide if you want treatment subsequent to an understandable explanation of the risks involved;
- have all your medical information kept confidential;
- withdraw consent for treatment at any time;
- obtain a second opinion;
- leave a hospital at any time (except if you have certain psychiatric conditions or have contracted some infections);
- be treated with care, consideration and dignity by caregivers;
- be fully informed of the costs of any medical procedure or treatment;
- look at any medical files from a caregiver or hospital;
- obtain legal advice about any matter arising from the treatment (at your own cost);
- exercise any of these rights on behalf of a child if you are the parent;
- ask to stay with a child at all times, except where separation is necessary for medical reasons;
- inform caregivers that you do not want to see, or speak to, a visitor or caller.

OK gents feeling radical? Grab those placards and repeat in an annoying monotonous way … 'What do we want? Patient rights! When do we want them? NOW!'

As a patient you have a responsibility to:

- know and disclose your medical history to caregivers;
- keep appointments with caregivers, or advise them if you can't make an appointment;
- inform caregivers if you are receiving treatment from another health professional;
- pay for any services and products received as a private patient, unless your insurance covers it;
- conduct yourself in a manner which doesn't interfere with the wellbeing or rights of other patients or staff;
- never be fully naked even with your partner mid-water birth. (As a male), you will be held to account by your caregiver should they be exposed to your tackle.

be called in to direct the care.

After the birth, your partner and baby will be cared for on a postnatal ward. Care will be provided by midwives and doctors – an obstetrician will be in the picture only if obstetric care is considered necessary. In some hospitals an early-discharge program will be offered. This is where your new family can go home early, if all is going well for your partner and the baby. A midwife will visit you in your home each day to check on your partner and baby to see how they are going until you are all ready to cope on your own.

As a public patient, all services provided are free under Medicare. Great, hey?

4. Midwifery-led Care in a Public Hospital

As a public patient you can opt for care by a small team of midwives at home or in a more home-like environment in a hospital (called a birth centre). The midwives who work in services like these tend to be very experienced and believe in a more natural approach to pregnancy and delivery. The small-team approach allows your partner to form a relationship with the midwives who will be providing care throughout the whole process.

Generally speaking, midwifery-led services are only offered to women who are healthy and don't present risk factors for complications. Midwifery-led care varies from place to place in terms of availability and what a birth centre has to offer, so contact your nearest public hospital for more information.

Care while pregnant and after the baby is born depends on the type of service available. Some midwife services are provided in your home, with an obstetrician check-up and tests provided at the local hospital. Others provide pregnancy care in birth centres. After the baby is born, care can be offered at home, in the birth centre or in a postnatal ward as a public patient.

This service is also free under Medicare. Sweet!

5. Shared-care GP in a Public Hospital

A shared-care GP is a doctor who has done a little bit of extra training to provide care during pregnancy. This doctor offers personalised service and is usually conveniently located near your partner's home or workplace. He or she will provide checkups and organise the tests your partner will need while pregnant. Your partner will have to attend the hospital for an assessment by an obstetrician.

Your GP will not be involved in the birth of the baby or supply postnatal care.

As with all other public patients, this service is free under Medicare.

6. GP Obstetrician

In regional and remote areas of the county, some GPs have taken on extra training to provide obstetric care to women in their communities. These doctors offer both public and private services, usually in smaller public hospitals.

Care while pregnant is the same as for a private obstetrician. Care usually takes place in the hospital clinic or in the GP's surgery. During labour care is as per private obstetrical, and care after the baby is born is provided by midwives (though the GP obstetrician will provide all further medical treatment required by your partner).

This service is free as a public patient, or, if private, as per a private obstetrician.

Single Caregiver Versus the Team Approach

According to a survey conducted by the Victorian government in 2000, one of the most important things women wanted in pregnancy was to know the folk providing their care. This is completely understandable. Pregnancy is a very intimate experience and it is only natural that expectant mothers would prefer not to be poked and prodded by a bunch of strangers! Knowing one's caregivers improves trust and increases a woman's confidence.

So, who provides the most personal service? Typically, those with the least number of caregivers; a no-brainer, when you think about it. From a midwifery perspective, the most intimate service is offered by a private midwife and any midwifery-led care in public hospitals. They offer one-on-one (or small teams) service throughout pregnancy, so the caregiver who looks after your partner in pregnancy will also help her through labour and teach her about baby care.

Obstetricians provide excellent one-on-one care during pregnancy, but are somewhat absent in labour and in the post-natal period. The shared-care GP offers not just initial pregnancy care but, if the vibe is right, care for the whole family after the show is over.

So, are teams bad?

In teams you may not get to know everyone. Having said this, however, even if your caregivers are strangers, bonds do tend to form quickly – especially in the throes of labour.

The care you receive from teams is generally friendly and professional, plus teams bring stacks of experience and expertise. Typically, the places where team care is provided are well re-sourced, with the ability to deal with most situations internally.

The following table provides a summary of the types of services available, and what they offer.

	Private midwife	Midwifery-led care	Private obstetrician	Shared-care	GP obstetrician	Public patient
Care in pregnancy	home or midwife's rooms	home or birth centre	doctor's rooms	GP's surgery & antenatal clinic	GP's surgery	antenatal clinic
Care in labour	home	home or birth centre	labour ward	labour ward	labour ward	labour ward
Care after birth	home	home or postnatal ward	postnatal ward	postnatal ward	postnatal ward	postnatal ward
Private/ public	private	public	private	public	private/ public	public
One caregiver or a team of caregivers?	individual	small team	team	team	small team	team

Private Versus Public

One thing that may have slipped your mind when thinking of having a baby is health insurance. A lot of people have private health insurance in Australia and may choose to use it when they are expecting a baby. In Australia, we have a nationwide

Aussie Birth Stats

The following facts are the most recent from the Australian Bureau of Statistics and prove one thing, there are a lot of babies out there!
- Australia recorded 301 000 births for the year ending 30 June 2009.
- Australia's total fertility rate reached a 30-year high with just under two babies per woman.
- This is the highest growth rate in 40 years (2.1% in 1969). On another note the CIA fact book, 2010, shows that in Australia 18.4% of the population is aged 0–14 years with 67.8% aged 15–64 years, so it appears we really need all these babies.

health system to provide healthcare free of cost to all citizens and residents. Some swear by using private insurance while others ask, why would you pay to have a baby? Both the private and public spheres have their advantages; we hope the following helps you decide.

As a private patient:
- your partner can choose a private obstetrician of her choice. At this stage she can't choose a midwife, but that might change in the near future.
- your partner can attend a private hospital to be cared for by her private obstetrician.
- your partner can attend some public hospitals as a private patient to be cared for by her private obstetrician. Sometimes she will need to share a room with others after the baby is born.
- private hospitals generally have single rooms, better food and more flexible visiting hours than public ones. They also tend to be smaller but not as well resourced.
- sometimes private insurance will not cover the full costs of doctor's fees and hospital costs, and you will have to pay the remainder.
- sometimes private jet with butler is available, just kidding!

As a public patient:
- your partner will be allocated her caregivers.

- generally she will attend her nearest appropriate public hospital.
- your partner may have to share a room with others after the baby is born.
- public hospitals, especially large ones, are well resourced and staffed.
- all medical attention is free for citizens and residents (and certain others – check the website of the Commonwealth Department of Health and Ageing to see who is eligible).
- private jets and butlers are not available in the public system, not kidding!

What Services Are Available Where You Live?

Not everyone in Australia lives within 10 minutes of a large city hospital and a café that does organic soy decaf moccachinos, so it stands to reason that some of the services offered for pregnant folk in larger places may not be available in regional and remote locations.

The following table has been included as a guide to the services likely to be available where you live. Make sure to check with your local hospital or health centre, as pregnancy services can vary greatly from place to place.

Available services by region		
Metropolitan	Regional	Remote
• Private midwife • Midwifery-led care • Private obstetrician/ private hospital • Shared-care • Public hospital	• Possible private midwife • Possible midwifery-led care • Possible private obstetrician/ private hospital • GP obstetrician • Public hospital	• GP obstetrician • Possible public hospital Women in remote areas who don't have access to a hospital may be moved to the nearest town (with a hospital) a few weeks before their due date.

Movin' On ...

If you thought that was complicated, consider that one day you may have to tell your son or daughter about the birds and the bees. Makes this stuff seem easy, really!

Useful Contacts

Cochrane Collaboration Consumer Network (VIC)
www.informedhealthonline.org
Tel: 03 9594 7530
Been told you need a certain treatment? Want the evidence
to ensure it's effective? Why not consult the experts at the
Cochrane consumer network!

**Royal Australian and New Zealand College of
Obstetricians and Gynaecologists (AUS & NZ)**
www.ranzcog.edu.au
Tel: 03 9417 1699
Good website about finding an obstetrician and for care
in pregnancy.

Australian College of Midwives (AUS)
www.midwives.org.au
Tel: 1300 360 480
For information on how to organise a midwife, and other
pregnancy-related information.

3

Fasten Your Seatbelts ...

The First Trimester Checklist

☑ Decide when you want to announce your pregnancy to the world at large.

☑ Know what to expect concerning changes in your partner's body.

☑ Know what to expect concerning changes in your partner's mood. (Read: beware!)

☑ Get a referral to the caregiver of your choice and offer support as your partner is pricked, prodded, scanned and generally scrutinised.

☑ Make some healthy changes to your lifestyle, and accept that some things are going to change, whether you like it or not!

☑ Make sure your partner takes her antenatal care record everywhere with her.

☑ Keep an eye out for serious health problems which may arise, but don't get anxious about them.
The chances of your partner having a healthy, problem-free pregnancy are high.

☑ Smugly contemplate the fact that you are now a small but important wheel in The Cycle of Life.

☑ Sit back and watch things grow.

L et's be frank, now that you're pregnant (or your partner, actually), you are most likely going to experience uncountable brain-numbing conversations about, you guessed it, *pregnancy*.

From the various bodily phenomena that you really don't want to know about (or distantly remember from school personal development classes) to the torturous act of leafing through a leaflet about prams (God help you!), a lot of this stuff isn't going to float your boat. This is why men in most societies automatically gravitate towards cooking meat at social events; it's genetic – they're practising their escape from any possible conversations of babies in the future. Really!

Beyond this you may find that there seems to be a strange fear factor at work. People tend to offer general congratulations, liberally spiced with the doom and gloom of Life After Baby (which sounds a bit like the title of a disaster movie). Well, fear not, having a baby is not unknown; as mentioned in Chapter 1, plenty of people have done it.

Here are a few of the things you're going to hear, and some responses you might make:

Your life's really going to change.

Oh really, tell me something I don't know?

It's expensive.

Bah, humbug, lots of things are expensive!

The sleepless nights!

No biggie; I used to voluntarily stay awake all night!

Now is the time to ignore the newborn nay-sayers and fearmongers and look at the positive side of things: you're going to be a god – oops, father.

For the first few years at least, your personal interests, be they stamp collecting, watching sport, trying to relax or a healthy personal vendetta, will be of great interest to your child. He or she will copy or join you in whatever activity you partake in, with cheerful readiness. When you think about it, it's a great thing to have someone interested in what you're interested in especially when your partner or friends really don't care. Face it: your partner and friends really don't care. You'll never find a bigger fan than in your own kid. (For the first few years, at any rate.)

So before your right-hand man or woman slinks off to parties, friends' houses or the shopping mall, make the most of it. You'll also gain respect. Your workmates, sports associates, intellectual peers, the dummies you deal with daily, your subordinates, your superiors, the guy driving up your arse this morning or that guy in IT who looks at you like you're simple whenever you ask a question, or, if you work in IT, that simpleton up in sales who asked you whether his DVD drive was a drink holder – all of them, and more you've forgotten about, don't respect you, don't see your true, deliberately understated genius. Your kid, however, will respect you and in fact take everything you say and do as gospel, even when you have no idea what you're talking about. Finally, some respect!

Beyond these positives, you will develop superhuman senses and strengths that non-dads, or people who don't know about the intricate art of nappy pinning, cannot appreciate. If a 727 is flying over (or, for that matter, through) your house while you are watching TV, your superhuman hearing will detect the whimpers of someone needing a bottle three rooms away. If there's a potentially fatal fall about to happen, you'll manage to grab your child and save him or her from certain doom – not as you see it happening but, more eerily, *before* you see it happening.

You're about to join an elite class of superhumans who all have their very own hero-worshipping fan club (admittedly comprised of only one person, who can't talk or walk), so enjoy it when it comes. It won't last long.

When to Announce It

Okey-dokey! Pregnancy successful, have clearly proven manhood. First thing to do, after hugging other half (who did her bit too) is to tell every person you have ever known your news. This includes arch-bastard work associates who you usually avoid talking to, and your local postman. It also doesn't hurt to accidentally include all those ex-girlfriends onto that group email you're about to send.

But wait, you're supposed to wait. Why? Although your decision about when to spill the beans is totally up to you, many couples decide to wait three months before going public, although an exception is usually made for close friends and family.

The main reason people tend to hold off from spreading the news is to make sure via prenatal screening that the baby is all right and everything is going to plan. Furthermore, the most common occurrence of miscarriages, which unfortunately are more common than most people think, is in the first three months.

In fact the statistical chances of miscarriage steadily decrease from the initial conception. For example, your partner's risk of miscarriage six weeks from her last period is approximately 15 per cent, this then drops right down to 1 per cent after 12 weeks.

Although there should be no embarrassment or stigma if the above does happen, many people wait because if there is a problem it may be a very personal and harrowing experience which they want to deal with in private or they are worried about putting other people in an emotional situation.

Your Partner in the First Trimester

In the 1957 science-fiction classic *The Incredible Shrinking Man*, an unfortunate bloke gets smaller and smaller after being exposed to a mysterious cloud of radiation. Your partner is about to become just the opposite: she's about to become The Incredible Swelling Woman (but rather than having been exposed to radiation, she's been exposed to, well … you!).

She will change in front of your very eyes, transforming from sexy woman into sexy human incubator. To help you prepare for what's to come, the following explains some of what the first trimester can mean for the inflating one.

Physical Changes in Your Loved One

Things will start to change pretty fast in your partner's body, and evidence of your manhood should start to show within two weeks of conception. Your loved one will start to morph in a number of ways that will instil in your heart a sense of wonder and make you repeat over and over again, 'Thank God I'm not a woman!'.

Breasts

As discussed in Chapter 1, in the first trimester you will notice your partner's breasts start to enlarge. This is caused by hormones preparing the breasts for milk production and delivery. You may notice that the areola (the area around the nipple) darkens and veins become visible, as more blood is sent to the breasts to get them ready for action.

The groundwork for milk production is being laid this trimester; however, your partner usually won't produce milk until week 16. Some woman might be sensitive about the changes to their breasts, so when you discuss them be diplomatic. And remember, handle with care!

Vagina

You may notice a white vaginal discharge in pregnancy. This is usually normal, but your partner may want to check with her caregiver to ensure it's not an infection. Added to this, sometimes a woman's vagina might turn bluish. This is known as Chadwick's sign and is considered normal.

Uterus

There are not many visible changes here in the first trimester, but by week 12 the growing uterus can be felt in the lower part of the abdomen. If you carefully feel your partner's belly you may discover a little bump just above the top of her pelvis. This is the uterus, and inside it is your baby.

Heart/Blood Flow

Your partner's heart is starting to enlarge as she deals with increasing demands on her body. By the end of the first trimester your partner's heart is working harder than ever before, circulating an extra 30 per cent blood volume and beating an average of 10–15 beats faster per minute than her non-pregnant counterpart. She is going for gold!

The Placenta

Voted ugliest organ in pregnancy and childbirth for eight years running, its foul looks disguise its incredible functionality. The placenta is fully developed by the end of the first trimester and is responsible for storing sugars, supplying oxygenated blood to the young foetus, removing carbon dioxide and releasing hormones. It also prevents harmful material reaching the baby through the placental blood barrier. If ever there was a case for not judging a book by its cover, this must be it.

Hormones

Hormones go crazy during the first trimester, which in turn causes physical changes to your partner's body. Internally, hormones are speeding up metabolism and helping her to store protein, fats and sugars to be used to build the baby.

These massive changes can cause fatigue and irritability, and you might be on the receiving end of the consequences of these. Suck it in, fellas, it's not you doing the hard yards! For more concrete advice on how to cope, read 'Managing Spontaneous Emotional Releases From Your Loved One' (pages 57–59).

• Stuff That May Stress Your Partner in the First Trimester

The first trimester is a time of rapid baby growth, surging hormones and psychological adaptation. For *both* of you to get through the first trimester unscathed, it's a good idea to have an understanding of some of the pregnancy stuff that may be distressing your loved one.

Cravings and Aversions

Pregnant women will crave all manner of weird and wonderful food combinations and it will be your job to buy or prepare them. Rice pudding with fried chips and tofu ice-cream can sometimes be hard to produce at any given moment, you can only do your best.

Cravings are thought to be the pregnant body's way of calling out for what it needs. If it needs vitamins it'll crave fruit, if it needs protein it'll crave meat, and so on.

The only cause to really be alarmed is if your partner starts craving strange things like dirt or cigarette butts (no kidding), in which case she may have a condition called pica and will need to visit a doctor (see opposite for more information on pica).

Pica

The name pica is derived from the Latin word for magpie, a bird renowned for its omnivorous feeding. The disorder is characterised by the eating of typically non-food substances (soil, coal or chalk, for example), or typically unappetising staples such as flour or raw potato.

Apart from ruining your next dinner party, pica can be harmful to both mother and child, as some things eaten in excess can be toxic.

Why would your pregnant partner want to eat stuff like that? Two major theories exist: the first is that pica is a result of hormonal/metabolic changes in pregnancy, and the second is that the embryo/foetus requires certain minerals and it makes Mummy get them, no matter what! Any signs of pica should be reported to your doctor.

Breast Tenderness

Yes, we know, we keep coming back to your partner's breasts, but can you really blame us?

From the second week your partner may develop a 'prickling sensation' as the blood supply to her breasts starts to increase. Around the six- to eight-week mark of the first trimester your partner's breasts increase in size and might become painful. To help overcome this:

- offer her a cold pack and/or paracetamol to help reduce pain and swelling, and
- handle breasts with care!

Morning Sickness

One of the more obvious complaints of pregnancy is morning sickness. As mentioned before, more than 50 per cent of pregnant women experience some level of nausea and/or vomiting between the fourth and seventh week following their last menstrual period. And no, as mentioned before, it's not confined to the morning.

For the overwhelming majority of women the condition subsides by the twentieth week of pregnancy. A rise in hormones such as chorionic gonadotrophin and oestrogen are thought to be the cause of morning sickness, as is enhanced sensitivity to smells.

Theories abound as to how your partner should deal with it, with some of the more accepted ideas being:

- your partner should eat small and simple snacks such as dry biscuits or fruit throughout the day, rather than having three big meals;
- your partner should avoid rich or spicy foods;
- your partner should avoid coffee;
- your partner should keep fluid intake up between meals rather than drinking with meals;
- ginger tea may relieve the problem;
- special acupuncture wristbands may relieve the problem.

If your partner's morning sickness is severe, she may have a condition called hyperemesis gravidarum (see 'Possible Serious Stuff to Worry About', pages 70–73). Get prompt medical attention if morning sickness seems excessive.

Bladder Issues

As your partner's uterus starts to expand it begins pressing and squeezing all the other organs in the abdomen, including the bladder. This may lead to more regular trips to the toilet.

Bladder issues can be reduced by slowing down on coffee and other natural diuretics (food and drinks that make you pee).

Fatigue

Fatigue is common from the fourth week of pregnancy and can last well into the second trimester. This can cause your partner a lot of grief, especially if she has commitments (like a job) that don't allow her to get any rest during the day. There are things that you can do to help, however:

- make sure your partner's nausea is well controlled (one study has suggested that women with high levels of nausea complained of similarly high levels of fatigue).
- give her the opportunity for a day nap, if possible.
- ensure she gets enough sleep at night.
- do the f#*%-ing dishes and let her put her feet up.

Moody Man Syndrome

www.commons.wikimedia.org/arjecahn
<http://www.flickr.com/photos/arje/>

Grumpy or a bit snappy with your loved one? It may just be that time of the month. A new study into mood swings in males suggests that men, like women, may suffer from fluctuations in hormone levels.

As reported in *New Scientist* magazine in 2002, Dr Gerald Lincoln of the Medical Research Council's Human Reproductive Sciences Unit in Edinburgh believes that mood swings in men, or 'irritable male syndrome' as it has been coined, may be due to stress levels, which cause a drop in the male hormone testosterone.

A correlation between behavioural changes in animals with lowered testosterone has already been observed in a type of sheep called Soay. The testosterone levels of Soay sheep rocket in mating season before disappointingly plummeting in the months afterwards.

Dr Lincoln followed eight rams and recorded how much they struck out irrationally or without provocation with their horns. The findings were that the lower the testosterone level, the more 'irritated' the rams seemed to be.

Dr Lincoln also observed similar patterns of behaviour in other mammals, including the reindeer and Indian elephant (presumably from a safe distance), and he surmised that the same thing may happen in human males: the lower the testosterone, the more prone to irritability.

Although it's probably a little early in the piece to use the hormonal excuse that half the world does when they're having a bad day, you've got some hard graft ahead, so it may be worth a try.

• Managing Spontaneous Emotional Releases by Your Loved One

OK, let's get this over and done with. Don't mention this within 20 kilometres of a woman, pregnant or otherwise, and definitely don't mention this loudly in a public place. No emails, phone conversations, texts – don't risk it. In fact, rip this page out and eat it as soon as you've read it.

Pregnant-woman Translator

'Maybe'	'No'
'Yes'	'No'
'No'	'Not on your life'
'No way'	'If you do that, I'll kill you'
'You want'	'You want!'
'I want'	'I'm having'
'We need'	'I'm having'
'I'm sorry'	'You'll be sorry!'
'You're sorry?'	'You'll be sorry!'
'You have to learn to communicate!'	'Just agree with me!'
'Are you listening to me!?'	'Too late, you're dead!'
'We need to buy a cot'	'We need to renovate the whole house.
'Put the cot there'	'Not there, you idiot, *there*!'
'What should we call him/her?'	'What am I going to call him/her?'
'What do you want to do?'	'We're doing what I want to do, no arguments!'
'I'm OK'	'Of course I'm not OK, you fool'
'I'm tired'	'You did this to me!'
'I'm sore'	'You did this to me!'

Women, as we are well aware, have a tendency to occasionally be irrational and, well, downright *moody* at times. As you know, and often forget, these 'periods' of time are often fairly short and quite predictable, and taken with a grain of salt and with a bit of forethought can be negotiated relatively easily without permanent harm to yourself or your psyche.

In pregnancy, and particularly in the first trimester, it is best to expect the unexpected. Your partner's moods and behaviour may oscillate wildly, leaving you confused and a teeny bit vulnerable. Sometimes these moods may be attributed to physical symptoms of pregnancy, like nausea and fatigue, and at other times you might be labelled as the cause (justified or not). Although totally unfathomable, this kind of scenario is likely to be more prevalent if you do things that will obviously annoy your pregnant partner – things like drinking until 3 a.m., playing too much golf, not cleaning, leaving your undies on the floor, or – God help you – saying, 'Yes, your bum actually does look big in that!'

However, be warned, if you're not doing the above, you're probably going to cop it anyway. Walking through the front door, sitting, speaking, the simple act of breathing or just being you, may be the catalyst for havoc.

Always remember, guilty or not, no matter how ridiculous or just plain loopy your partner's logic may be:

- don't take it personally;
- don't fight back – take it on the chin, go and wash the dishes;
- think: this is short term – try to pacify the situation, don't become engaged;
- have flowers handy at all times;
- even if you can't follow the conversation, at least pretend to listen to what is being said (just say, 'God you are beautiful, even when you're angry!');
- accept the fact that with all the changes going on in her body, hormonal and otherwise, your partner may be anxious about the future and need a bit more reassurance than usual from you;
- try and use humour to defuse the situation (ha!);
- and of course, try a little empathy: find out if she is sick, tired or in pain, and do something to help.
  If all else fails:
- assume the foetal position in the boot of your car or some other place where you're unlikely to be found for a day or two.

On a serious note if you feel your partner's mood swings are out of control you should talk to her about them. If you are still worried try to get her to a doctor and if at any time you feel she is a danger to herself or others take her to your local hospital's emergency department.

Lifestyle Changes

Had Ian Dury been in your situation at the time it would have been a very different song.

Sex and drugs and rock and roll … and diet … and medication … and alcohol … smoking … and coffee.

Sex Life

Do you want the good news or the bad news first?

OK, the good news is, if you have a normal sex life, in a normal pregnancy, then sex is safe to have at all stages of the pregnancy. However, there are some things (like a low placenta) that can stop you having penetrative sex. Your partner's caregiver will tell you

Staying Sexy

In 2003 www.babycenter.com queried the sexual habits of 'the largest group of new and expectant parents ever assembled on the planet'. The online survey questioned 20000 willing participants (17000 women and 3000 men), uncovering some interesting, albeit sometimes horrifying, facts about the effects of pregnancy and children on a couple's sex life.

In the overall pregnancy stakes, 40.2 per cent claimed nothing much had changed, which is fine if you had a lot of sex before pregnancy. Conversely, 40.3 per cent noted that they might as well have been sleeping in separate beds, with only 19.4 per cent saying they were still going at it hammer and tongs.

In terms of actual rises or falls in desire, the odds seem a lot more promising: 39.7 per cent claimed a rise in sexual desire at some time in the pregnancy, with 21.7 per cent noting increased desire in the second trimester. A dip in desire was reported by 30.2 per cent of the participants, while 30 per cent stayed on an even keel. Not a ring-in, but the odds ain't too bad.

In the post-pregnancy stakes, things are unfortunately looking better for the bookie.

Although 88 per cent of participants claimed to have sex some time in the first four months after pregnancy, the big picture seems a bit grimmer: 30.4 per cent claimed not being able to get it together at a time when both were in the mood, 23.2 per cent said they would rather sleep in separate beds, and 19.7 per cent described sex as the ever-elusive Holy Grail. The main reasons given for a lack of interest in sex were decreased sex drive, lack of time, insecurity about body image and tiredness.

On the upside (fingers crossed), 19.1 per cent said becoming a parent hadn't changed their sex life much, with a very lucky 7.7 per cent claiming that parenthood was like an aphrodisiac.

if it's an issue. But remember if you can't have intercourse you can always have outercourse!

Now for the bad news. Sore breasts, fatigue, nausea and likely vomiting probably aren't the best ingredients for a sultry night in. Most mothers-to-be find that their sexual desire fluctuates throughout pregnancy. Some women (hopefully yours) become highly motivated for sex at certain times of pregnancy, while others don't at all.

All in all, however, you're probably going to have to come to terms with the fact that your pre-pregnancy hanging-off-the-chandeliers sex life is going to be over for a while.

So listen up, because no one else is going to tell you this. If sex is on offer (from your partner, of course) and you're feeling a little tired from a week at work or there's a football final on, take the offer and enjoy it. It might be the last for a while.

Love is all fun and games until someone loses an eye or gets pregnant.
Jim Cole

Vices

Your DNA has joined the gene pool: hoorah! Some of your characteristics – your hair colour, height and bad teeth – will be blessing or troubling future generations of your descendants until the end of time. When you think about it, it's kinda like living forever. However, before any of this can happen, you and your partner need to have a cold, hard look at your lifestyle to make sure it won't affect your little bundle of joy.

Being pregnant is an occupational hazard of being a wife.
Queen Victoria

Medications

Some drugs can have undesirable effects on the embryo/foetus in pregnancy, so you need to see if it's still safe for your partner to take her regular medication while pregnant. Discuss this with a GP or your caregiver.

Recreational Drugs

The basic fact is that any use of recreational drugs in pregnancy is really bad. If your partner has a drug addiction or is still using recreational drugs while pregnant, you are headed for a world of pain, so see your health provider and get some help, pronto!

Recreational drugs are an issue in a number of ways. They can cause:

• miscarriage and other serious complications in pregnancy;
• birth defects in a growing bub;
• addiction for newborn babies.

Smoking

If your partner smokes, or is exposed to passive smoking in pregnancy, she is not just hurting herself but is also harming her unborn child. (It actually says this on the pack!) Smoking in pregnancy, or exposure to passive smoking, has been shown to increase the chance of babies coming early (a major health risk for them), small babies and babies with lung problems. It also increases the chances of miscarriage and stillbirth.

So, if your partner smokes she needs to see a health provider to help her quit or limit the damage that smoking can cause. Or if you smoke around her, obviously it's time to stop!

Diet

We are what we eat ... but in your baby's case he or she is what your partner eats. She needs a good diet to make sure your baby has the right things to grow up to be the right stuff!

It's not rocket science, gents, just make sure your partner eats well and gets enough carbohydrates (bread, rice, pasta, noodles), calcium and fat-soluble vitamins (milk, yoghurt, cheese), plenty of fruit, vegetables and legumes (you know, beans and peas), and protein (meat, fish, eggs).

One thing that is very important to have in your diet is folate (Vitamin B). It helps babies grow normally. As we mentioned in the first chapter it is found in grains, dark green vegetables, fruit and fruit juice, potatoes, beans and Vegemite. If eating enough of these foods is an issue your partner should see her caregiver and maybe start dietary supplements.

Because of the risk of listeria infection in pregnancy, your partner needs to avoid certain foods, including unpasteurised dairy products, seafood and raw meats (see 'Possible Serious Stuff to Worry About', pages 70–73).

Alchohol

Alcohol causes a range of problems that can seriously affect the health of your growing baby. The issue is that alcohol is a teratogen – a substance that can lead to abnormalities in an embryo or foetus (in severe cases this effect is known as Foetal Alcohol Syndrome). This is particularly relevant in the first trimester because the placenta is immature and its protective qualities are not fully developed. Also, the baby is undertaking very rapid growth in this period.

So, how much alcohol can your partner safely drink in the first trimester? There is conflicting evidence about this, but the current recommendations suggest that a mother avoid the demon drink altogether. This applies not just in the first trimester but throughout the entire pregnancy. So lock up the drinks cabinet and hand over the car keys, because we all know who is going to be the designated driver for the next nine months!

Caffeine

Caffeine, the wonder drug that has been keeping our hospitals, transport system and police force functioning for years, is sadly not good in excess during pregnancy. Recent research has shown that having too much caffeine can increase the risk of miscarriage. It is thought that a daily intake of greater than 200–300 mg can cause problems.

Here is a list of common stuff that contains caffeine. You do the maths!
• ground coffee: 100 mg caffeine per 250 ml cup;
• instant coffee: 75 mg per 250 ml cup;
• tea: 50 mg per 250 ml cup (medium strength);
• hot chocolate made with cocoa: 50 mg per 250 ml cup;
• cola: 35 mg per 250 ml cup.

Interestingly, many women go off coffee when they get pregnant anyway.

♦ Your Baby in the First Trimester	
Weeks 1–5	Although no longer a glint in your eye, the fertilised egg is but a speck in your partner's womb during this period. But while small, the creature who will eventually hog the sofa or argue with you about the length of her miniskirt is very busy. Gender has already been determined and the embryo has implanted itself into the uterine wall, ready to grow. The uterus, incidentally, will increase its capacity 1000 times before this is all over. Glad it's not you? At the end of four weeks the embryo is only about 2 millimetres in length, about the size of the oversized full-stop at the end of this sentence, and looks a bit like a tiny sculpture by Henry Moore. While the bub may still be tiny, it is mighty: by the end of week 4 a primitive nervous system has developed, and the human heart has begun to form and starts to beat. (OH MY GOD, IT'S ALIVE!) At this stage your baby is called an embryo.
Week 6	Your little dude or dudess is about 1.3 centimetres in length, and details such as nostrils and eye lenses are starting to appear, which are always handy. The brain is also starting its long journey to developing 100 million neurons, and rather than looking like a blob your future child now looks like … well, a sort of prawn-shaped blob.
Week 7	Fingers, toes and elbows are on the go and it's starting to look like a baby, admittedly a very alien-like baby with external genitalia present.
Week 8	Cartilage and bone, along with eye structures, are forming. Your kid is about 1.6 centimetres in length and weighs about 1 gram.
Week 9	Your little alien–prawn–monster thing can now officially be called a foetus.
Week 10	Things are starting to function: the kidneys start to work and the foetus starts to pass urine (into your partner's abdomen – eeeeeoooh!). The bub also starts to suck and swallow fluid (including its own urine – double eeeeeoooh!). It is now able to start curling its fingers around things, and fingerprints are forming.
Week 11	Things are starting to look more human-like, and all systems are go, with more structures and organs beginning to function. A fine wispy hair called lanugo has appeared all over the foetus's body, and hair and nails have appeared. On average the bub is now 4.1 centimetres long and weighs 7 grams.
Week 12	The baby's intestines have started to get going and should be filling with their first poo – how cute. Vocal cords are also beginning to form. The foetus is now moving freely around but is so small that its movements can't be felt by the mother. The baby has laid down the building blocks for adaptation to life outside, and at about 5.4 centimetres is well on the way to becoming your bouncing bundle of joy!

Thalassaemia and Sickle Cell Anaemia

Although potentially debilitating, the hereditary diseases thalassaemia and sickle cell anaemia are fascinating in terms of their evolutionary biology and our relationship with them. The diseases are caused by the inheritance of recessive genes and have the strange character of being both a blessing and a curse to the individuals and populations they affect: carriers of the recessive gene are given a biological advantage in resistance to malaria, while those who have both recessive genes inherit a potentially fatal blood disease.

Sickle cell anaemia causes red blood cells to change to a crescent or sickle shape, which obstructs their movement through the body, resulting in clogged blood vessels and limiting supplies of oxygen. Normal red blood cells break down after about four months before being absorbed back into the bloodstream. Sickle cells, however, break down after only ten to 20 days, causing anaemia.

The red blood cells of people carrying the single recessive sickle cell gene tend to turn sickle shaped when infected by the malaria parasite. When these cells pass through the spleen they are culled because of their odd shape. This process rids the body of the parasite faster, while at the same time giving the infected individual a much better chance of survival from malaria. In contrast, those who have inherited both genes for the disease from both parents contract the full-blown, and often lethal, disease.

Medical Stuff in the First Trimester

The first trimester is awash with check-ups, tests and appointments. Regardless of who is going to care for your partner through her pregnancy, the initial stuff that you need to get done can be organised by a GP. By the end of week 12 the following should be organised.

Blood Tests

After your partner's pregnancy has been confirmed at the GP's with a blood test, the doctor may want to do some other blood tests. These could include:

- **Blood group** – good to know in case of bleeding that might lead to the need for a blood transfusion;

- **Rhesus factor** – assesses for Rhesus disease (see page 103);
- **Full blood count** – looks at the cells to check for infections and other problems;
- **VDRL** – a blood test for syphilis;
- **Rubella immune status** – checks for immunity to rubella, which can cause defects in a growing baby;
- **Hepatitis B & C screen** – checks for Hep B & C, both of which are bad for babies;
- **HIV** – checks for the virus which causes AIDS;
- **Thalassaemia screen** – checks pregnant women of Mediterranean, Middle Eastern or African origin for a genetic disease of the blood that may cause severe anaemia (if result is positive, you may also need to be tested).

The Dating Scan

If you want, ask your GP to organise a dating scan. Some folk opt to have a dating scan, others don't. The idea is that a scan will provide an accurate estimate of when the baby is scheduled to make its debut.

The Nuchal Translucency Scan

If your partner is 35 or over (or if she wants it, regardless of age), you can ask your GP or caregiver to organise a nuchal translucency scan. This is a test for Down syndrome. It doesn't tell you if your baby is affected, rather it estimates the risk that your baby has of the disorder.

The test has two parts: (1) a blood test at around 10–13 weeks of pregnancy that looks for certain proteins that might be present in Down syndrome, and (2) a specialised ultrasound performed at 11–13 weeks of pregnancy. This scan measures the folds of skin around the back of the neck of a foetus. Differing measurements can correlate with the risk of Down syndrome.

If a problem is detected, you might want some more definitive testing organised.

Meet Your Caregiver

By the end of week 12 you should have had a consultation, called the booking visit, with your chosen caregiver. (Make sure you have obtained a referral from your GP and made an appointment to see your caregiver in good time prior to your visit.) Your caregiver will normally provide information about the service they provide, answer your questions, ask a lot of questions of their own, and perform a short-ish physical examination on your partner.

The following stuff is normally explored in your booking visit, but variations exist, depending on what service you guys have chosen.

1. Social History
This basically involves a series of potentially embarrassing questions about your personal lives. In the public system your caregiver believes they have a responsibility to assess the social wellbeing of pregnant folk and identify people who might have a problem with money, drugs or other social problems. Thus as part of the booking visit your caregiver will ask a series of personal questions about your partner's sexual past, the drugs either of you may take, everyone's mental health, and your financial situation. At some point during the booking visit you'll most likely be wondering why on earth they need to know all this. Good question. Apart from enjoying making people squirm, your caregiver is looking for signs that you guys need some assistance with your personal life, and if necessary will unleash a horde of well-meaning people to provide it.

2. Obstetric History
This involves yet another series of really embarrassing questions, but this time about your partner's obstetric history. This is very important for identifying problems which might arise later on. Things that might interest your caregiver include the incidence of past miscarriage or stillbirth, terminations of pregnancy and any other previous pregnancy problems.

3. Past Illnesses
Since your partner's body is the crucible for the new life of your growing bub, it stands to reason that any ill-health she may have experienced may affect the progress of her pregnancy.

Your caregiver may be looking for some of the following in terms of the pregnancy and possible precautions that may need to be taken:

- previous deep venous thrombosis (a blood clot, usually in the legs);
- pulmonary embolism (a blood or air clot in the lungs);
- heart conditions;
- high blood pressure;
- any kind of chronic illness;
- any problem with the uterus;
- smoking or alcohol/other drug use;
- diabetes;
- psychiatric problems;
- any blood disorders.

4. Family Illnesses

While you're probably familiar with the concept that your extended family can be bad for your mental health, you may not know that your relatives and in-laws can also affect your baby's physical health. Certain illnesses in pregnancy have a genetic link, thus your family's genetic history is explored by your caregiver to look for red flags to identify problems. These may include a family history of hypertension, diabetes or mental illness.

5. Physical Examination

Your caregiver will usually put your partner over the pits to make sure all's well.

Among other things, blood pressure, temperature, heart rate, height of uterus and your partner's weight are measured. This provides a base line to compare your partner's progress on future visits.

The Antenatal Care Record

At the booking visit or at your GP's, your partner will receive an antenatal care record. This is a card that carries information about what care your partner has received, plus scan and blood test results and the like. This document is used by all the people involved in the pregnancy. As such it is a complete record of

Heteropaternal Superfecundation

Actually harder to believe than pronounce, heteropaternal superfecundation is the production of fraternal twins from two different eggs, fertilised at different times by two different sperm, from, wait for it, two different men!

Although extremely rare in humans, there have been a number of cases observed in the past. One of the earliest cases was reported in 1810 by Dr John Archer, who claimed that a woman who had had sex with a black man and a white man, within a short period of time, had produced both a white and a bi-racial twin. A more recent study published in 1994 in the *Journal of Forensic Science* reported two cases confirmed through blood testing, one occurring as a result of group sex.

If you're thinking this would be a good plot for a soap opera, then you're too late. *DOOL* (that's *Days of Our Lives*) have used heteropaternal superfecundation as a storyline with one of their characters, Sami Brady, already.

everything and is essential in places like emergency departments or labour wards should something unexpected happen (touch wood). The idea with these cards is that they go everywhere your partner goes, not just to her appointments. You have an important job here, and that is to make sure that if she goes to work, to the movies or to Timbuktu, she takes the card. Period.

Care Timetable	
Weeks 0–5	• Organise to see a GP
Weeks 6–8	• Confirm pregnancy via blood testing • Discuss nutrition and health in pregnancy with GP • Blood tests for: blood group and antibody screen, full blood count, VDRL, rubella, hepatitis B & C, HIV and thalassaemia • Discuss and book dating scan and nuchal translucency scan if you have decided these are a good idea • Get a referral to your caregiver • Get an antenatal care record
Weeks 8–12	• Have first booking visit with caregiver

Possible Serious Stuff to Worry About

OK guys, this section is likely to totally freak you out, but it's a case of better the devil you know. The majority of pregnancies run smoothly; however, it's an unfortunate fact of life that bad stuff can happen. So, as the protector and advocate of your partner you need to be aware of the things that can go wrong. Read on, and remember: knowledge is power.

Listeria

It is a creepy fact that microbes have colonised almost every environment on the planet. From the hot vents of deep-sea volcanoes to your lower intestine, they're there, multiplying by the millions, growing, doing their thing.

One common bacteria is called *listeria* and it is found in the food we eat. Unpasteurised dairy products, raw or undercooked fish, meat and pre-cooked chilled foods can all contain *listeria*.

When a healthy adult is exposed to this bacterium it is not an issue, but in pregnancy, in the newborn or with folk with a compromised immune system, *listeria* can be deadly. *Listeria* infection has been linked to premature birth, stillbirth, meningitis (brain infection) and septicaemia (blood infection), and can lead to maternal death.

Symptoms of *listeria* infection include fever and headaches, tiredness, aches and pains, and possibly nausea and diarrhoea. If you are concerned that your partner has been infected, seek medical advice.

In pregnancy, the best way to avoid a *listeria* infection is by avoiding high-risk foods and by taking care with food preparation. The foods that your partner should steer away from are:
- unpasteurised dairy products, both cow and goat (this includes cheeses such as brie, camembert, ricotta, feta and blue-vein cheese);
- raw seafood, as in sushi and sashimi, oysters and shellfish in general (unless they have been thoroughly cooked);
- cold meats, pâté and other meat spreads;
- pre-cooked ready-to-eat meals;
- any other re-heated foods.

When preparing food such as raw meat, fish or vegetables, exercise good kitchen hygiene and cook the food properly.

Bleeding in Early Pregnancy

Generally speaking, vaginal bleeding in pregnancy is of concern and must be checked out. Too much bleeding may be a sign of a miscarriage or other serious problems, so you both need to be aware of it and take the necessary actions if it happens.

If there is any bleeding before the twentieth week of pregnancy it is better to be safe than sorry: get it diagnosed and managed by getting to your local emergency department. If your partner has lots of bleeding (far greater than her normal period), with or without dizziness/fainting, sweating, racing heartbeat, nausea or confusion, don't muck around – get an ambulance.

Ectopic Pregnancy

This occurs when the embryo implants itself in the wrong place, usually in the fallopian tube and not the uterine wall. This condition usually develops between weeks 4 and 12 and is relatively uncommon, affecting only 1.5 per cent of all pregnancies.

As the baby develops and enlarges, the fallopian tube can rupture, leading to bleeding, shock and, in rare cases, maternal death. Because the bub is in the wrong place, nothing can be done to save it, but it's game on to save your partner.

Diagnosis is simply a matter of performing an ultrasound to see if the embryo/foetus is in the uterus. If it's not there, it's in the wrong place!

I've got seven kids. The three words you hear most around my house are 'hello', 'goodbye', and 'I'm pregnant'.

Dean Martin

Ectopic symptoms to be aware of are severe abdominal pain, with or without any of the following symptoms:
• vaginal bleeding;
• shoulder-tip pain;
• abdominal swelling;
• dizziness/fainting;
• confusion.

If these symptoms occur, get your arses to your nearest emergency department posthaste. (You might think about calling an ambulance for this one, gents.)

Risk factors include:
• previous ectopic pregnancy;
• previous sexually transmitted diseases;
• use of intrauterine contraceptive devices;
• congenital abnormalities of the female reproductive system.

It is said that the present is pregnant with the future.

Voltaire

Hyperemesis Gravidarum

Known more commonly as hyperemesis, this condition is like ordinary morning sickness on steroids, and needs to be taken seriously, as it can cause damage to both mother and baby. Symptoms include repeated vomiting, weight loss and dehydration. If your partner shows any of these symptoms, take her to your local emergency department. Hyperemesis may require a period of hospitalisation.

Movin' On …

With all this talk of disease and possible problems, you're probably thinking the first trimester should be called the 'I'm-a-paranoid-mess trimester'. In actual fact, that's probably a better name for the third trimester …

But fear not, the majority of pregnancies and births occur without problems, and it's not like you're the first person in the world to have to go through the process.

Just keep an eye out for the possible problems mentioned in this chapter, but most of all, enjoy it: you're going to be a father. What's more, you'll soon be heading into the second trimester – often called the party trimester – and things should start to get a whole lot easier.

Useful Contacts

ACT Drug Information Service (ACT)
Tel: 02 6244 3333
Provides telephone information about drugs in pregnancy in the Australian Capital Territory.

Alcohol and Drug Information Network (AUS)
www.adin.com.au
Tel: 03 9278 8100
Provides information about alcohol and recreational drugs and contact details for drug and alcohol assistance services throughout the country.

Australian Department of Health and Ageing (AUS)
www.healthinsite.gov.au
This Australian government website offers a range of advice and up-to-date information on pregnancy, birth and care of your new baby.

Babycenter (AUS)
www.babycenter.com.au
This website is sponsored by Johnson & Johnson and has a lot of good general pregnancy and newborn baby information.

Cochrane Collaboration Consumer Network (VIC)
www.informedhealthonline.org
Tel: 03 9594 7530
Been told you need a certain treatment?
Want the evidence to ensure it's effective?
Why not consult the experts at the
Cochrane consumer network!

Monash Medical Centre (VIC)
Tel: 03 9594 6666
Provides telephone information about drugs in pregnancy in Victoria.

MotherSafe (NSW)
Tel: 02 9382 6539
Provides telephone information about drugs in pregnancy in New South Wales.

National Prescribing Service (AUS)
www.nsp.org.au
Tel: 1300 633 424
Provides telephone information about drugs in pregnancy Australia wide.

Nutrition Australia (AUS)
www.nutritionaustralia.org
Tel: 03 9650 5165
Provides information on diet and pregnancy.

Royal Women's Hospital (VIC)
www.thewomens.org.au
Tel: 03 8345 2000
Provides information about drugs in pregnancy in Victoria.

Western Australian Women's & Children's Health Services (WA)
Tel: 08 9340 2723
Provides telephone information about drugs in pregnancy in Western Australia.

Women's and Children's Hospital (SA)
Tel: 08 8161 7222
Provides telephone information about drugs in pregnancy in South Australia.

4

It's Party Time!
The Second Trimester Checklist

☑ Your partner will be booking her 18–20 week morphology scan, so arrange time off work so you can be there.

☑ Discuss with your partner whether you want to know the sex of the baby.

☑ Start discussion with your partner about maternity and paternity leave – what are you entitled to and when to start.

☑ Break out that flared disco suit from your hey-day look at it and put it away again, you won't be needing it for a while.

☑ Arrange a wild party at your place starting at midday and raging on till the wee hours of the afternoon.

☑ Sometime in the trimester have a major stress-out over the money you both will need to spend.

☑ Towards the end of the trimester, feel the baby kick!

OK, you've probably already gathered that the second trimester, the so-called 'party trimester', doesn't involve you and your partner dancing around semi-naked, waving glow sticks as the morning sun glints through a debauched haze (ah, those were the days!). No, the 'party' bit refers to the fact that most of the discomforts of your partner's early pregnancy should have subsided, and she (and you) will have sort of got used to the whole pregnancy thing.

It's a quiet time, a time to cautiously relax, a time to enjoy the moment – a bit like being in the eye of a cyclone, really. Added to this, this is the time when your partner has hopefully taken on that wholesome pregnancy glow, or 'bloom', unique to women with a bun in the oven. Her hair and skin will have taken on a lustrous glow, and she should be in good spirits.

Cost of Children

A 2002 report commissioned by AMP called 'All They Need is Love and Around $450000' sounded more like a ransom demand than a research paper. As the title suggests the report put the cost of raising two children to the age of 20 at about $448000. AMP's next report, 'Honey, I Calculated the Kids ... it's $537000', published in 2007, paints a similar picture. In a nutshell the study showed that expenditure on children is clearly tied to income, with wealthier families spending more on their offspring.

The report divided incomes into three groups: Low income at around $729 a week; middle income at around $1538 a week; and high income at $3216 a week, making the average Australian income $1722 a week.

Low-income families spent an average of $65 a week on one child from the age of 0–4, while high-income families spent more than double at $225 a week; middle-income families spent $132 a week on the same age group. These costs rise pretty much exponentially as the child gets older. In the age group of 15–17, high-income earners spent $433 a week, followed by middle-income earners at $271 a week, and low income earners at $180 a week.

Two children obviously cost more, but take refuge in the fact that economies of scale do seem to kick in as clothes and toys can be handed down, and because families simply cannot afford to spend the money they did on the first child. Averaged across all age ranges, two children cost

So there you have it: your partner's happy, you're happy, everything's cruising … until, of course, you think about *money*. These days kids aren't cheap, and if your partner works there's probably going to be minus one income for a period of time (or perhaps forever). If she doesn't work then you're going to have to come up with the goods –

FOR THE TERM OF YOUR NATURAL LIFE.

So at this stage it's probably worth assessing the family finances, taking into account the fact that there's going to be an extra person to feed and buy iPods for. Probably the best thing to do is write up a budget. Baby budgets are similar to your normal, everyday, run-of-the-mill budgets apart from two glaring differences.

$231 per week for low-income families; $366 for middle-income families; and $607 for high-income families.

The study also tried to give an idea of where all this money might be going, with the figures differing radically depending on what income bracket a family was in. Housing, food (There are children starving in Africa!); transport (When I was young I used to walk 10 miles to school!) and the mysterious 'other' (Damn you Xbox!) were the highest costs, in descending order for low-income families with two kids. In contrast, from most expensive, education, food, recreation and transport were the biggest costs for high-income families.

You'll be glad to hear that the validity of these studies has been questioned by Mike Dockery, Associate Professor in the School of Economics and Finance at Curtin University of Technology. In his 2009 study, 'Measuring "the Real" Cost of Children: A Net Wealth Approach', Dockery reckoned that children cost 'at most' $1300 per annum, and may even lead to an increase in net wealth.

His study, based on almost 3200 couples, compared the net wealth of couples with and without children, rather than just the overall amount spent on raising children. The results were that couples with children seemed to accumulate wealth more quickly than those without, and have a higher percentage of home ownership.

Firstly, there are a bunch of baby things you won't ever have thought of (but your partner will have) which tend to drive up the 'OUT' column. Strangely, the prices of these things will mysteriously match the price of that new surfboard, TV or gadget you had been saving for.

Secondly, if your pre-baby budget included a second wage, there's more than likely going to be less money than usual to pay for all that baby paraphernalia.

My problem lies in reconciling my gross habits with my net income.
Errol Flynn

Budgeting for a Baby (Read It and Weep!)

One of the main factors in preparing a budget when expecting a newborn is to ensure that you and your partner get together to draw it up. Sounds obvious, but if one person is budgeting while the other is … well, *not* budgeting, you are probably going to run into problems.

Accounting for the Baby

The baby is going to need a fairly extensive list of things that you'll need to include in a budget, so it's a good idea to write these things down and estimate the costs now (see 'Stuff to Get', pages 119–120).

I'm living so far beyond my income that we may almost be said to be living apart.
E.E. Cummings

Track Your Income

The key to any successful budget, baby or not, is to successfully track what is coming in and what is going out. As mentioned before, with a baby budget there is usually a lot less coming in and a lot more going out. Once you have worked out exactly where your money is going you can then agree with each other about what you can cut down on – be it not buying lunch at work, or walking instead of driving the car – this is where your savings will come from.

Once You've Done a Budget, Keep Reviewing it

Although everyone's budget strategy will be different, the core concept of any budget is being able to predict your expenses ahead of time and change your spending behaviour accordingly. So once you've decided on a budget, review it at regular intervals to make sure you're sticking to it.

Save Now

If you haven't already put money aside, start saving now. It's a good idea to lie low and save as much extra money as possible before the baby is born. This will come in very handy if one of you stops work to become the home carer, and it will also help to furnish the baby with those initial essentials.

Parental Leave

Another thing to be aware of is parental leave – in particular your rights when it comes to any leave you or your partner may wish to take.

The term 'parental leave' includes maternity, paternity and adoption leave. This has been included as a core minimum condition of the Australian Pay and Conditions Standards. Unpaid leave of up to a maximum of 12 months can be accessed by a woman and/or her spouse on the birth or adoption of a child. To be eligible for parental leave, you or your partner have to have worked for your employer for 12 months or more previous to the date of the birth of your baby. You need to give your employer written notice of your intention to take parental leave at least ten weeks before the anticipated start of that leave.

Your partner's employer cannot dismiss her if she is pregnant, or if either of you has applied for maternity or paternity leave or are on maternity or paternity leave. After the period of parental leave has expired, the employee has a right to return to the same job, or an equivalent one in status and pay. An employee must also give notice of his/her intention to return to work.

If your or your partner's employer does not meet their obligations, a formal complaint in writing can be lodged with Fair Work Australia. The complaint will be investigated and the employer may be prosecuted and fined.

Casual Employees

Eligible casual employees are entitled to parental leave. An 'eligible casual' is one who has been:

(a) employed by an employer on a regular and systematic basis for several periods of employment, or on a regular and systematic basis for an ongoing period of employment during at least 12 months; and

(b) who has, but for the pregnancy or the decision to adopt, a reasonable expectation of ongoing employment.

Dad Time

As far as paid parental leave goes, a 2006 survey released by the Equal Opportunity for Women in the Workplace Commission sheds some light on what is on offer.

Of the 1443 organisations surveyed across Australia, 32 per cent offered some sort of paid paternity leave (which is more than double the 15 per cent offered in 2001). Of these, 67 per cent offered one week, 16 per cent two weeks and 7 per cent six weeks. For all other offerings up to 14 weeks, no more than 4 per cent of companies offered paid leave.

Although there are no statistics available on the percentage of men who take unpaid paternity leave, evidence suggests that it is low. A government report published in 2004 cited a number of reasons for why few men take unpaid paternity leave. Not surprisingly, the 'unpaid' part of 'unpaid leave' was one of the main issues, with money – or lack of it – being a major hurdle.

The study also examined less obvious reasons for men being reluctant to take leave, including the idea that paternity leave adversely affected a man's career, and that cultural expectations associated with men and their role as breadwinners also held men back. Finally, workforce pressures played a part in limiting the uptake of paternity leave, with increased work hours and lack of job security being major factors.

If you feel a bit ripped off with the lack of paternity leave on offer in Australia, then perhaps a move to the far northern hemisphere is the answer. The Swedish government stipulates that a compulsory three months of the 16 months paid leave on offer must be taken by the minority parent (or primary earner), which is in most cases the father.

You have to wonder if Swedish ski resorts have crèches.

Short and Long Paternity Leave

Parental leave conditions may vary slightly from state to state within Australia, so you should check the terms of leave with your local government.

New fathers can take up to 52 weeks continuous unpaid leave if they are the primary caregiver, called 'paternity leave', or up to one week unpaid leave if they are not the primary caregiver, called 'short paternity leave'.

Australia's Paid Parental Leave Scheme

Probably a bit late for some, the Paid Parental Leave (PPL) scheme commences on 1 January 2011. For those having babies due after that date, here's what you're entitled to:

- an eligible person will receive taxable PPL payments at the level of the Federal Minimum Wage (currently $570 a week before tax) for a maximum period of 18 weeks. In most cases, the person will receive the payment through their employer.
- to be eligible for the PPL scheme, the primary carer (usually the mother) must be in paid work and:
  - have been engaged in work continuously for at least ten of the 13 months prior to the expected birth or adoption of the child; and
  - have undertaken at least 330 hours of paid work in the ten-month period (an average of around one day of paid work a week).

If the primary carer earned more than $150000 in the previous year they are not eligible for PPL.

PPL will cover employees, including casual workers, as well as contractors and the

If it can't be fixed by duct tape or WD-40, it's a female problem.
Jason Love

Life is tough enough without having someone kick you from the inside.
Rita Rudner

self-employed. If a primary carer returns to work before they have received all of their PPL entitlements, they may be able to transfer the unused part of their PPL to another caregiver (usually the father) who meets eligibility requirements.

Eligible families can choose whether to participate in the scheme, depending on their individual circumstances. Families electing to participate in the scheme will not receive the Baby Bonus (except in multiple-birth cases) or Family Tax Benefit Part B during the 18-week PPL period. The 'dependent spouse', 'child housekeeper' and 'housekeeper' tax offsets also will not be available during this period.

New mothers who are not eligible for PPL will continue to receive, if eligible, the current forms of family assistance (including the Baby Bonus).

Should You Find Out the Sex of Your Baby?

So, now all that finance stuff is over and done with, let's get on with the interesting stuff … Nowadays, the widespread use of ultrasound technology has offered expectant parents the opportunity to find out whether they should paint the nursery blue or pink.

In the second trimester, at around the 20-week mark, your sonographer should, with a fair degree of accuracy, be able to identify the sex of your little one. So, what should you do? Should you find out the sex of your baby or leave it as a surprise? Let the debate begin … !

The Case for the Affirmative (Let's Find Out Now!)

Not generalising at all, but many of us have experienced the fact that women don't always like surprises. Many an engagement ring spontaneously given to a woman is secretly modified at a jeweller's, while clothes bought on a whim by a loving boyfriend are often exchanged.

So if your partner claims to not want to know the sex of the baby, perhaps deep down she may … Good luck teasing this one out!

On a more serious note, it can be an excellent thing to know the sex of the baby. If you are the sort of people who need to be

Folklore Methods of Determining Sex

Stuck at home watching a chick flick with your dear one? Why not surprise her with something different by road-testing the following traditional methods of finding out the sex of the baby.

The Wedding Ring Method
Tie a strand of your partner's hair (if it's too short, just use cotton) to her wedding ring, or some other favourite ring. Hold the hair with the attached ring as still as you can over her abdomen or wrist. If the ring starts to move from side to side, it's a female; if it spins, it's a boy.

The Belly Shape Method
Supposedly the shape of your partner's abdomen in late second and third trimesters can predict the sex of your unborn baby. To work it out, look at your partner's abdomen while she is standing in profile. If her tummy is rugby ball shaped, it's a boy. Soccer-ball shaped, it's a girl.

The Heart-rate Method
Boys aggressive, girls calm and logical ... so the theory goes, and supposedly this is also the case while they're still baking. Meaning that male babies have a faster heart rate than their female compatriots.

During a routine antenatal visit, ask your caregiver what the baby's heart rate is. If greater than 140 beats per minute, your child is supposedly a bloke; less than 140 beats per minute, a girl.

The Chinese Calendar Method
Simply consult this calendar (page 107) constructed by Chinese wise-men and soothsayers and discover the sex of your baby. It must be true!

(or want to be) organised, knowing the sex of the baby can get you started. There's the nursery to paint, clothes to buy, names to shortlist and schools to consider. So go and find out.

The Case for the Negative (No Way, Let's Keep It a Surprise!)

Everything today is explained, controlled and quantified, but thank goodness there is still the odd surprise in life. One of the greatest surprises you can have in life is to wait until your baby is born to discover the sex.

You remember the joy of unwrapping your Christmas presents as a kid? Remember that feeling of expectation in the

The Kwolu-aatmwol Sex Switchers

In the sunny highlands of Papua New Guinea, home of fearsome tribes, tropical jungles and the Kokoda Track, things are not what they seem. The Sambia people have borne witness to an amazing phenomenon they call Kwolu-aagtmwol, whereby some girls become male during puberty.

These 'girls' are in fact blokes with an endocrine disorder called 5-alpha-reductase deficiency. This magical substance, 5-alpha-reductase is used in the male body to convert testosterone into dihydrotestosterone, a hormone which develops our secondary sexual characteristics (the five o'clock shadow, to name but one).

Boys with this disorder are often born with female-looking genitalia and internal testicles, and as a consequence in the Sambia society are brought up as girls. However, you can't hold back nature, and during puberty some strange stuff starts happening to Daddy's little girl! The clitoris enlarges and becomes a penis; the testicles, hidden from view for so long, finally descend to their God-given place and start to produce sperm. Along with this, facial hair starts to develop and they begin to bulk up.

When the Kwolu-aagtmwol 'become' boys they forget their crushes on the village lothario and become sexually interested in females, which causes some serious social rearrangements. With the 'new' boy now acting as a man, he must learn to drink, chase girls and procrastinate about mowing the lawn, like all the other men of his village.

And you thought your life was complicated.

pit of your stomach? You can have that all again if you wait to discover the sex of your baby.

On a more practical note, while identifying the sex of your baby via ultrasound is pretty accurate, it's not foolproof. Imagine someone telling their family and friends they are having a girl: they're fully prepared for the arrival of their little princess, with name, room colour and girly clothes all sorted out … and then out pops a big, bouncing boy! At least those in the keep-it-a-surprise camp don't have to suffer that embarrassment!

Ultrasound Technology

Your partner will be interested to know that both sonar fish finders and the ultrasound machine used to view your bub use the same technology of imaging high-frequency soundwaves to create real-time images. Bats, dolphins and whales also use a similar technique, called echolocation, to navigate.

So how does the ultrasound actually work?

It transmits high-frequency soundwaves into your partner's body using a probe. These soundwaves bounce back when they hit boundaries between fluid and soft tissue, or tissue and bone. The probe then reads these echoes, which are travelling at the speed of sound, and translates the differing distances through the minute differences in time that the soundwaves take to return. The result is a two-dimensional image of a foetus; in fact, your child to be!

Twins and More

Another big issue which might come up while having an ultrasound is that you may find out, to your initial horror, that you're going to have twins or, God forbid, triplets, or quadruplets, or quintuplets, or sextuplets, or … you get the picture. If this happens, sit down and remember to breathe.

Feeling better? You now have an instant family to care for. This will mean:

- you may need to sit down for a year or so, but you won't be able to;
- it won't take a few strong drinks to make you see double anymore;
- you'll suddenly find 'two for one' offers really good value
- OK! Two kids, two hands … I can do this;
- your partner may need a different caregiver;
- she may need a caesarean;
- she may have a shorter labour, with a greater chance of premature birth;
- she will need extra help with breast- or bottle feeding;
- you will need to help out around the house and with the babies (but don't worry, in about eight years time you can put them to work, and you may never have to stack the dishwasher or unblock the toilet again).

Trippy Twins

Anecdotal evidence of mysterious similarities and unexplained 'feelings' between twins abound, but just how factual are these reports? The Minnesota Twin Family Study, which started in 1983 and is the largest study of twins to date, has attempted to look at twins in terms of nature versus nurture – with some surprising results.

One of the most intriguing examples from the study concerns the so-called 'Jim Twins'. Separated at four weeks of age and reunited at the age of 39, Jim Lewis and Jim Springer are identical twins with more than just physical similarities.

Jim Lewis and Jim Springer both had dogs named 'Toy', both had married a woman named Linda, divorced, and then married a woman named Betty, both had a son called James Allan and James Alan respectively, each had owned a light-blue Chevrolet, and both had identical tastes in beer and cigarette brands. The twins also had what is thought to be the same genetic predisposition to migraines, weight gain, sleeplessness and sinus problems.

Although the twins were also defined by many differences, these seemed to be outweighed by their uncanny similarities. Some scientists think that there is a whole lot more carried by our DNA than we have ever suspected, while others put the more inexplicable similarities down to cultural influences.

Probably one of the most striking discoveries in twin studies is that alpha waves, a kind of brain wave that can be plotted when a person is in a state of rest, are identical in identical twins, whereas most alpha waves are, like fingerprints, unique.

www.commons.wikimedia.org

Don't laugh, this could be you in a few months!

So what are the chances of getting twins? The number of twins born in Australia increased from one in 100 births in 1980 to one in 65 births in 2000. Unfortunately there are no current statistics but it's pretty clear the trend is up, with the rising use of fertility treatments seeming to be the cause. Twins (and more) are classified as either monozygotic, or coming from one egg (which makes them identical), or dizygotic, or coming from two or more eggs (which makes them fraternal).

Monozygotic, or identical, twins come about when one egg and one sperm come together to form a cell which divides, creating two genetically identical individuals. Generally monozygotic twins look alike, but fine physical details such as fingerprints will be different. Statistically, identical twins are more likely to be girls.

Mirror twins occur in approximately 25 per cent of identical twins. These twins develop reverse asymmetric features – for example, birthmarks may appear on opposite sides of the body. How mirror twins are made is a mystery to modern science.

It is not economical to go to bed early to save the candles if the result is twins.

Chinese Proverb

Tales From the Crib

As reported by the BBC News on Thursday 8 May 2003, a Brazilian woman with two wombs gave birth to twins, one from each womb.

Apparently about 1 in 1000 women are thought to possess twin wombs; however, the chances of two babies coming to term in two wombs is extremely rare.

Extraordinarily, a British woman, Hannah Kersey, aged 23, gave birth to triplets from two wombs, in December 2006. One womb supplied identical twins Ruby and Tilly, while Grace was born from the other womb. The chances of this happening were given at about 25 million to one.

Dizygotic, or fraternal, twins come about when two eggs and two sperm come together, creating two genetically different individuals. Their similarities are limited to looking like brothers or sisters.

Your Partner in the Second Trimester

Your loved one continues to change in the second trimester. Although some things like fatigue and morning sickness may have settled down, there are some other things that may give her curry.

Physical Changes to Your Loved One

Now your partner has hit the second trimester the changes to her body become more noticeable. As her abdomen swells she becomes a walking pregnancy billboard advertising her pregnancy to all. Don't be surprised if complete strangers corner her on the street and discuss the most intimate details of their birthing experience.

14th century illustration of 'Dorothea', who allegedly gave birth to undecaplets (that's 11) after having given birth to nonuplets (that's nine) And you thought you were struggling!

Breasts

In the second trimester, your partner's breasts continue to swell and by week 16 she should start to produce colostrum, the first milk. In our culture where breasts are often a sexual rather than a nutritional symbol, this can be a bit confronting for all concerned!

Uterus

The uterus grows approximately 1 centimetre per week as it expands to keep pace with the baby's development. By week 20, the top of the uterus should have reached your partner's belly-button and she should start to feel the baby move – a sensation described by some women as small bubbles of gas, or butterflies.

While the uterus is growing, the uterine walls start to thicken and soak up a heap of your partner's extra blood: an extra 100 millilitres per minute is pumped by the end of the first trimester, increasing to 500 millilitres per minute by the end of the pregnancy.

Usually by the end of the second trimester you should start to feel your little Chuck Norris's punches, kicks, twists and turns. To feel the way of the dragon, ask your partner to tell you when the baby is moving and then rest your hand gently on her abdomen.

Heart

Anatomically speaking, your partner has more heart now than she has ever had. By the end of the second trimester her heart has grown larger and is working hard. It's now pumping like a champion race horse.

The heart's muscle layers have increased to assist with the increased demands of the growing foetus, and it's moving an extra 30 per cent of blood. As the baby increases in size, your partner's heart is pushed away from its normal position upwards into the chest cavity. While this sounds alarming, it's all part of Mother Nature's plan. Yes gents, she has a big heart; but it's in the wrong place.

Hormones

By the middle of the second trimester the nausea and tiredness associated with pregnancy usually settle down. However, the hormones relaxin and progesterone, which cause muscle relaxation, have an increased presence in the second trimester of pregnancy. This, for some women, can lead to back and muscle ache (see 'Back Pain', page 92). Oxytocin (the love drug – see 'Physical Changes in Your Loved One', page 123) and prolactin also start to produce breast milk.

The Placenta

The placenta is now fully functioning and doing a great job. However, it can occasionally cause some problems (see 'Placental Abruption', pages 102–103, and 'Placenta Praevia', page 134).

Amniotic Fluid

The fluid in which your child floats is comprised of 99 per cent water and 1 per cent dissolved baby foods and wastes. As mentioned in Chapter 3, the bub swims in the amniotic fluid, drinks it, pees in it and drinks it some more – a bit like a kids' swimming pool, minus the band aids.

In times of crisis the amniotic fluid acts as a shock absorber, taking the impact of bumps and blows. It also moderates the baby's temperature and provides some nutrients. Otherwise known as liquor, it's as golden in colour as its namesake and is all-round great stuff!

• Stuff That May Stress Your Partner in the Second Trimester

While this is the party trimester and things should have settled down somewhat, unfortunately you're not out of the woods yet. No nausea or fatigue, maybe, but as her belly grows there are some other things that may upset your loved one. So read on and be alert, but not alarmed!

Back Pain

Despite the best of intentions of men, women throughout the world still do most of the housework, and while you may think this is an agreeable arrangement, be careful that your loved one doesn't do too many domestic chores or undertake any heavy lifting, as there is a possibility that she may develop crippling back pain.

Back pain in the second and third trimesters is generally due to three factors: increased hormone levels (relaxin and progesterone), increased weight from the bub, and your partner's attempt to maintain pre-pregnancy domestic and work commitments with a rather full belly.

Never more true, the adage 'prevention is better than cure' is the name of the game here, so to ensure your partner doesn't blow a gasket, do the following:
• suggest she works on her posture and stands as tall as possible (no slouching!);
• make sure she avoids lifting heavy or awkward objects;
• make sure she sits in a chair that supports her lower back while at work or in the home.

If she *does* get occasional back pain:
• get her a hot pack or some paracetamol;
• get off your arse to save her back!

Important! If back pain won't go away, or comes and goes in a regular pattern, this might indicate more serious issues like placental abruption or preterm labour which may need to be assessed at a hospital or by your caregiver.

Leg Cramp

Leg cramp is caused by the spontaneous contraction of the calf muscles and is yet another of the minor problems your long-suffering pregnant partner may face.

It is thought that low sodium and calcium levels and high phosphate levels might be to blame, so a dietary change may be required that will increase calcium and sodium. Add a little more salt to her diet, and some milk or other dairy foods too. This should hopefully correct the problem.

It is, however, a good idea for your partner to get calf/leg pain checked out by her caregiver on the off-chance she has developed a blood clot in the leg.

The Cold War, Pregnancy and Gymnastics

Sounding like a horror movie set in the bleak setting of Cold War Russia, this actually *is* a horror story set in the bleak setting of Cold War Russia!

Although not many shots were fired between America and the USSR, the battle for global dominance was fought in all areas of human endeavour, and in gymnastics there were casualties. Unfortunately for talented Eastern bloc gymnasts, doctors from the USSR discovered that during pregnancy more red blood cells were produced, allowing for greater muscle strength. The doctors also surmised that the hormones progesterone and relaxin produced in pregnancy led to a more supple body.

The obvious conclusion was to get the country's top gymnasts pregnant. As pint-sized gold medallist Olga Karasyov remembered in a German television interview in 1994, 'The team were forced to become pregnant shortly before the 1968 Olympics … Girls that did not have a boyfriend or husband were made to have sex with their coach.' Then, after ten weeks, the girls were forced to have an abortion. Refusal to comply with this program led to being thrown off the team.

Dark times, huh?

Bleeding Gums

Some women may develop bleeding or swollen gums during pregnancy. This is thought to be caused by the hormone oestrogen. The most immediate fix is to get a softer toothbrush. If you're still concerned, get your partner to go visit the dentist and ask him or her to check it out.

Constipation

Blame the hormone progesterone. While it's doing its job relaxing the muscles in the back, pelvis and other areas, it's also relaxing the bowels, which can cause constipation. Treat this by ensuring an adequate intake of fluids and an increased consumption of fruit and vegetables. Like all problems mentioned in this book, if constipation doesn't settle down, see your caregiver.

Lifestyle Changes

The second trimester brings changes in lifestyle for both your partner and yourself. There's a possibility that you both may be feeling like sex as the discomfort of the first trimester may have abated plus it's a great time for your partner (and yourself) to get fit and healthy in an effort to make the pregnancy as smooth as possible.

Sex Life

As discussed in the last chapter, having sex isn't going to harm the baby. Added to this, the second trimester is likely (hopefully) to be a period when your partner is more interested in sex.

Now that the classic missionary position is impeded by a speed hump, the major factor in having sex when your partner is pregnant is to find a comfortable position that won't put pressure on her uterus or belly. Unfortunately, this leaves the good old sex-on-a-moving-motorcycle stuff out of the question for now.

Popular positions to limit pressure on your partner's belly may include the following.

The Spoon

This position, in which the man cradles the woman from behind, is a goodie, as there is no pressure placed on the abdomen. (A spoon is not actually involved, unless used to eat ice-cream. Could be interesting …)

The Side by Side
Also limiting pressure on your partner's abdomen, this position allows for a bit more physical contact than the spoon position, as you're front on – which has its benefits. Two of them, actually.

The Woman on Top
This position, as the title suggests, has the woman on top, limiting abdominal pressure and allowing for better depth of penetration. A variation on this position is the 'reverse cowboy', where the woman faces the opposite direction, with similar advantages. These positions may become a bit tiring for your partner in later pregnancy, however.

The Rear-entry Position
This position allows your partner's tummy to hang free and can be adapted to an 'edge-of-the-bed' position. The variation involves your partner kneeling by the side of the bed and cushioning her torso on the bed's edge with a pillow, while you stand or kneel behind. The position boasts better penetration, G-spot stimulation and quite a good view.

Your pre-pregnancy bedroom athleticism is probably going to be over for a while.

Exercise
Right, break out the sweatbands, put on the '80s aerobics DVDs and let's get physical! Your partner should try to stay fit during pregnancy, and a good way to achieve this is to share an exercise routine with her.

It is suggested that a pregnant woman try and do at least 30 minutes of non-strenuous exercise, like walking or swimming, every day. It is worth noting that certain pregnancy complications may rule out physical activity, so make sure your partner checks with her caregiver before she embarks on a fitness regimen.

For a pregnant woman, some of the benefits of exercise include:
- helping her to relax;
- keeping her healthy;
- assisting in easing back pain;
- helping to prepare for labour.

• Your Baby in the Second Trimester	
Weeks 12–14	Your little bundle weighs approximately 110 grams and is about 12 centimetres long by the end of week 14. During this period the foetus starts growing muscle in a period of accelerated growth that would turn body builders green with envy. While the foetus is piling on the pecs, it continues to grow the fine lanugo hair all over its body. In this period, the bub's oral palate comes together in preparation for giving you lip when it's older.
Weeks 14–16	By the end of this period the foetus weighs approximately 250 grams and is about 14 centimetres long. Weeks 14–16 begin a period of facial readjustment. The eyes move from the side of the head into the face and the ears move up from near the jaw to the correct anatomical position. The bub's skeleton has formed and would now be visible in an X-ray. (Not that you're going to do that.)
Weeks 18–20	Growth slows down a bit during these weeks as baby takes a breather. By the end of week 20 it weighs about 460 grams and is approximately 19 centimetres long. The babe's skin is now covered by a greasy substance called vernix caseosa, which looks strangely like cream cheese. This helps protect the baby's skin from the amniotic fluid (if a grown man can get wrinkled skin in the bath after one hour, think of the wrinkles after nine months!). The head and eyebrow hair are now visible (OMG, not a mono-brow?!), and foetal movement should now be felt by the mother.
Weeks 20–22	At week 22 the baby weighs 630 grams and is 21 centimetres long, give or take a bit. Brown fat, a special baby energy source, has begun to get laid down, ready for use later on.

Weeks 20–22 (continued)	Surfactant, the amazing detergent-like substance that stops our lungs from sticking together like a 20 cent deflated balloon at a kid's birthday party, starts to be produced in its tiny lungs. Skin appears red from blood vessels just below the skin's surface. It is at this point, I'm sorry to say, that your baby is a living definition of the word ugly. Yep, it has fallen from the ugly tree and hit every bloody branch on the way down!
Weeks 22–24	Your baby weighs approximately 820 grams and is 23 centimetres long by week 24. It has regular periods of sleep and responds to noise ('Can you guys shut the f#*% up, I'm trying to rest in here!'). Towards the end of this period, babies have some chance to survive if born.
Weeks 24–28	At week 28 the baby weighs roughly 1300 grams, is about 27 centimetres in length and starts to practise breathing. The baby's nervous system can now control its body temperature. White fat, a longer-term energy source, is laid down, and the baby's bone marrow starts to produce red blood cells. The lanugo disappears from your child's face (thank Christ!) and your little one no longer resembles Rasputin (or his famous bearded sister). By 28 weeks, survival can be expected if the bub is born without other complications.

Medical Stuff in the Second Trimester

With all the 'partying' and finances to organise this trimester it's important to remember there is still medical stuff to do. One of the really cool things to do medically speaking is listening to the baby's heartbeat with a device called a foetal Doppler.

Antenatal Appointments

In the second trimester your partner's care is predominantly provided by your caregiver, with your loved one attending regular check-ups and having a few important scans, tests and other things. Each caregiver does things slightly differently, but usually the following is done during the antenatal visits:
• your partner's weight will be regularly taken;
• her urine will be tested;
• her blood pressure will be taken;
• measurements of uterus growth will be recorded;
• the foetal heartbeat will be listened to;
• any problems or issues your partner might have will be discussed.

The Doppler Effect

A foetal Doppler is used for monitoring the heart rate of a foetus. Monitoring the baby's heartbeat is extremely useful in assessing the condition of the baby. It uses the so-called 'Doppler effect' to do this.

The basis of the Doppler effect is that there is a change in frequency of a wave for an observer moving relative to the source of the wave. This is best explained by using the example of a person listening to an ambulance. As the siren approaches, passes and recedes, its sound changes, because the frequency of the sound changes according to its distance from the person listening.

To 'hear the heart' of your baby a handpiece is applied to the abdomen of your partner. It emits millions of ultrasonic soundwaves per second and these travel through the amniotic fluid, slip through the baby and bounce off the little one's moving heart or flowing blood. These soundwaves return to the handpiece and are interpreted as a heartbeat! Neat huh!

The Doppler effect occurs because the frequency of the soundwaves produced by the same source can be changed by the motion of the source, or even by the observer or both at the same time.

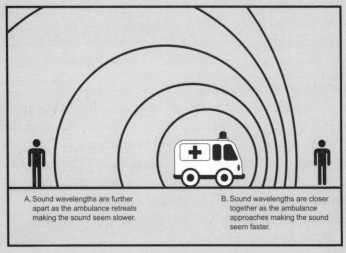

A. Sound wavelengths are further apart as the ambulance retreats making the sound seem slower.

B. Sound wavelengths are closer together as the ambulance approaches making the sound seem faster.

If you do not attend antenatal visits with your partner, spare a thought for her. While you are at work, joking with colleagues and taking long lunches, she will probably be sitting in a doctor's waiting room or an antenatal clinic (with its walls covered by government posters demanding safe sex in the gay and lesbian community), watching daytime TV, waiting, waiting and waiting to be called.

Tests and Scans

The Glucose Tolerance Test

This tests for a problem in pregnancy called gestational diabetes.

1. The 50 gram test for women not at risk

This involves your partner waking up in the morning and drinking a sugary drink. She then has her blood tested for glucose levels. If the result is high, she may have to do a more specialised test, called the 75 gram test.

2. The 75 gram test for women at risk

Your partner follows a special diet for three days, then, 8–12 hours before testing, only drinks water. She then drinks a sugary drink and has her blood taken twice usually at a two hour interval. If her blood sugar reading is high, your partner may have gestational diabetes and may need special treatment (see 'Diabetes in Pregnancy', page 101).

The Morphology Ultrasound

Your partner may have had a dating scan and/or a nuchal translucency ultrasound back in the first trimester, which may or may not have been of much interest to you. However, the morphology ultrasound, which occurs at around 18–20 weeks, is definitely something to be interested in, as you will actually get to see the little tyke for the first time. You can also find out the sex of your baby, if you so choose.

So, without sounding like a big girl's blouse, this scan is an amazing experience and you should get there! No amount of uptight bosses, lazy subordinates or other work commitments should make you miss this one. It's magic.

Apart from blowing your mind, the morphology scan is important because of the following:

- your baby's body systems are given a once-over;
- the size and weight of your baby are estimated;
- the position of the placenta is determined (see 'Placenta Praevia', page 133);
- multiple pregnancies may be diagnosed ('What the f#*%!');
- any possible problems or congenital defects may be identified;
- the sex of the baby (and no, that's not the penis, it's the umbilical cord) can be determined.

Vaginal Swab

Your partner's caregiver may want to see if your partner has been colonised by a bacteria known as group B streptococcus. Group B streptococcus is a common household-variety bacteria that grows in, and on, lots of people. It has, however, been linked to serious illness in new babies.

To identify those pregnant women who have the bacteria, a vaginal swab is taken. Some caregivers take two swabs, one in the second trimester and one closer to full term, while others only take one around 24 weeks. If the bacteria is identified, your partner can be treated with antibiotics during labour in order to protect the newborn baby.

Care Timetable	
Weeks 12–18	• More blood tests: blood group and antibodies (see Chapter 3) • A 75 gram glucose tolerance test for those at risk of getting gestational diabetes
Weeks 18–20	• Foetal morphology ultrasound scans (see above)
Weeks 20–24	• Vaginal swab • Still more blood tests: full blood count and antibody screen (see Chapter 3)
Around 24 weeks	• A 50 gram glucose tolerance test for folk with a low risk of developing gestational diabetes
28 weeks	• Anti-D injection, if required (see 'Rhesus Disease', page 103)

Possible Serious Stuff to Worry About

There are some medical issues in the second trimester that can be a bit nasty. But don't stress out too much as most pregnancies go to term without a hitch and even if a problem was to appear it will usually respond to treatment. As a partner the best thing you can be is informed, so read on gents and remember ... 'Be alert but not alarmed'.

Diabetes in Pregnancy

The jury is out about the cause of diabetes in pregnancy. What *is* generally accepted is that women who have high blood sugar can have large babies, and that this might pose problems for the mother when it comes time for her baby to make its grand entrance into the world. Furthermore, women who have high blood sugar in pregnancy can develop diabetes in later life.

If your partner has gestational diabetes she will probably be referred to an endocrinologist. In practical terms, she may need to:

- make dietary changes to reduce carbohydrates;
- have more frequent scans to determine how big the baby is as the pregnancy progresses;
- have injections of insulin to reduce her blood sugar;
- (possibly) have a caesarean if the baby is large.

Hypertension in Pregnancy

Hypertension, or elevated blood pressure, can affect the wellbeing of both mother and child. It usually develops from around 20 weeks and is broken into numerous sub-classifications, depending on its severity and effects. During pregnancy, any blood pressure above 130/80 is cause for concern.

Pregnancy-induced hypertension can affect your partner's kidneys, liver and the placenta, and have an impact upon the growth of the baby. In the worst cases it can be life-threatening for your partner and baby. So it's important that you don't ignore the signs of high blood pressure. These are:

- excessive puffiness in the hands, feet or around the body;
- headaches;
- dizziness;
- blurred vision or visual disturbance;
- abdominal pain.

Get your partner to see your caregiver if you have any of these symptoms. Depending on its severity, hypertension is treated by anti-hypertensive drugs and may require hospitalisation.

Bleeding in Later Pregnancy

Vaginal bleeding from 24 weeks onwards is called an antepartum haemorrhage and, as you might suspect, needs to be urgently checked out. The two main causes of bleeding in the second trimester are listed below.

Note that if your partner experiences any of the following symptoms then she needs urgent medical attention:

• a lot of bleeding;
• dizziness/fainting;
• sweating;
• racing heartbeat;
• nausea;
• confusion.

1. Placental Abruption

This is a serious problem where the placenta separates (either partially or fully) from the wall of the uterus. It can occur from about the twentieth week of pregnancy. Causes can include hypertension, pre-term rupture of the membranes, previous placental abruption, accidents, smoking and cocaine use. A placental abruption deprives the baby of the oxygen and nutrients carried in the mother's blood. It can also cause severe illness in the mother.

Signs of placental abruption might be:

• symptoms of hypertension;
• firm/hard abdomen;
• abdominal pain;
• signs of blood loss;
• dizziness/fainting;
• sweating;
• racing heartbeat;
• nausea;
• confusion.

Seek medical attention immediately if your partner shows any of these symptoms.

Depending on the severity of the abruption, a blood transfusion and a possible emergency caesarean may be necessary.

2. Blood-clotting Problems

Sometimes a pregnant woman may develop problems with her ability to develop blood clots. This can relate to a pre-existing disease, or problems caused by blood pressure or liver disease.

Rhesus Disease

As part of her antenatal care your partner will be tested for the Rhesus factor, or Rh factor. This is a knot of proteins that sit on the outside of some people's red blood cells. If the baby has inherited the Rh factor from the father and the mother doesn't have it, her immune system sees the baby's blood cells as a threat and attacks them – which, quite obviously, is a major problem. But as serious as this sounds it is totally treatable, simply with a couple of injections of a fantastic substance called Anti-D. Anti-D injections are routinely given at around 28 and 34 weeks, and just after delivery of the baby, or additionally if your partner has vaginal bleeding.

Antenatal Care 35 +

Sarah from the Bible gave birth at 50, and an IVF mother from Italy did it at 65. However, without divine or medical intervention, some women find it difficult to conceive and maintain a normal pregnancy as they advance in age. In the world of obstetrics, women who are 35 and older are offered a range of tests and services not routinely offered to those of a younger age.

Although it may seem a case of out-and-out ageism, there is sound evidence to support the need for the extra care provided for those 35 years and over.

If your partner has crossed that line in the sand she has an increased risk of:
• diabetes in pregnancy
• early birth and miscarriage
• having a child with genetic abnormalities (like Down syndrome)
    Just how great are the risks?

Diabetes in Pregnancy 35 +

Data from the Commonwealth Department of Health and Ageing shows the risk of being diagnosed with gestational diabetes increases with age – from 1 per cent among 15–19-year-old women, to 13 per cent among women 44–49 years of age.

If your partner is 35 or older, she may be offered earlier testing and the more extensive 75 gram test for diabetes in pregnancy.

Pre-term Labour 35 +

Pre-term (early) birth is bad for a baby's health and wellbeing. While teenage mothers have the greatest risk of pre-term labour, the second demographic at risk of early labour are women over 35. Statistics from the American National Center for Health show that:

- 35–39-year-old mothers were almost 15 per cent more likely to have a premature baby than mums in the 25–29-year age bracket;
- women aged 40 and over were almost 50 per cent more likely to have their baby early when compared with women in the 25–29-year age group.

If your partner is 35 or over, she may be offered more frequent visits to your caregiver in later pregnancy.

Down Syndrome 35 +

Age is also a factor in the incidence of Down syndrome, which, caused by an extra chromosome, is one of the most common causes of intellectual disability. As the table below shows probability of the syndrome increases rapidly with age.

Down Syndrome Statistics	
under 25 years	1:1500
30 years	1:900
35 years	1:380
40 years	1:110
45 years	1:30
50 years	1:6

Screening and Diagnostic Tests for Chromosomal Disorders

First of all, let it be known that by far the vast majority of pregnancies in Australia come to term without any major problems or inherent diseases, so there's no need to get neurotic about things.

As we have seen above, the risk of having a child with a chromosomal disorder like Down syndrome increases with maternal age, but it is not only women over 35 who need further testing for genetic or chromosomal problems. Younger women may have been notified of a high probability of a problem from a routine nuchal transluceny test in the first trimester, for example; other women may have a hereditary disease that runs through the family and therefore they require further tests.

If there is a substantial risk that your baby has a problem, it's important to obtain counselling before undertaking testing. This can usually be provided by or organised through your caregiver. It is important to understand the advantages and disadvantages of having a screening test or a diagnostic test, and any further testing that may be offered.

So, what tests are available?

Screening Tests

Screening tests don't diagnose a problem; they offer a statistical probability that the foetus may have a problem, so you can then decide if you want to undertake any diagnostic tests. On the upside, screening tests don't tend to have any associated risks concerning possible harm to the foetus, but on the downside, they don't diagnose problems with certainty, giving only statistical probabilities.

Screening tests include blood or serum tests and a variety of ultrasound scans. If screening tests *do* indicate a substantial risk of having a foetal problem, you may decide to consider further diagnostic tests.

Diagnostic Tests

If screening tests come back with a high risk of an abnormality, you and your partner can elect to have diagnostic testing. Diagnostic tests are able to clearly diagnose whether or not the foetus has a problem. However, they are also invasive and therefore present a minor chance of miscarriage.

The tests involve obtaining a small tissue sample from the placenta, the amniotic fluid or the umbilical cord blood to diagnose a problem. The main diagnostic tests include chorionic villus sampling (CVS), amniocentesis and cordiocentesis. All have disadvantages relating to the dangers of miscarriage.

Diagnostic testing is usually performed by a reproductive medical specialist in a clinic, either through the public or private system. Your partner and baby may need to be monitored for complications for a short time afterwards.

The screening of the foetus and the possible outcomes of such screenings may throw up some of the most difficult moral questions that you and your partner will ever have to deal with. Screening and diagnostic tests basically deal with the identification of foetal abnormalities which, if detected, offer parents the opportunity to make some difficult decisions about their unborn baby. It is vital that you and your partner are both aware of your choices and their implications, and are able to openly discuss your feelings on these matters before any decisions are made.

Get as much information as possible so that you and your partner can consider all available options. Get access to counselling as soon as possible so that you can get assistance in deciding what the most appropriate option will be. If the choice is to continue the pregnancy, support and information is important before, during and after the birth of the baby. If the choice is not to continue with the pregnancy, all aspects of the termination need to be discussed, including the support available before and after the hospital stay.

Movin' On ...

Whoa, the party's finished, they're turning off the lights and you can't believe the bar's already closed. Yep the relative calm of the second trimester passes pretty quickly and before you know it you are already moving into the third and final trimester.

You're heading down a one-way road to parenthood now buddy, your old life passing by like signs on the highway to places you think you've been to before ... but can't remember!

Chinese Pregnancy Calendar

The following predictor chart of the Chinese Pregnancy Calendar provides an indication of the gender of the baby. Follow the steps below the calendar to make your prediction of the baby gender.

	Jan	Feb	Mar	Apr	May	Jun	Jul	Aug	Sep	Oct	Nov	Dec
					Chinese Pregnancy Calendar							
18	Girl	Boy	Girl	Boy	Boy	Boy	Boy	Boy	Boy	Boy	Boy	Boy
19	Boy	Girl	Boy	Girl	Girl	Boy	Boy	Girl	Boy	Boy	Girl	Girl
20	Girl	Boy	Girl	Boy	Boy	Boy	Boy	Boy	Boy	Girl	Boy	Boy
21	Boy	Girl	Girl	Girl	Girl	Girl	Girl	Girl	Girl	Girl	Girl	Girl
22	Girl	Boy	Boy	Girl	Boy	Girl	Girl	Boy	Girl	Girl	Girl	Girl
23	Boy	Boy	Boy	Girl	Boy	Boy	Girl	Girl	Girl	Boy	Boy	Girl
24	Boy	Girl	Girl	Boy	Boy	Girl	Boy	Girl	Girl	Boy	Boy	Girl
25	Girl	Boy	Girl	Boy	Girl	Boy	Girl	Boy	Girl	Boy	Boy	Boy
26	Boy	Boy	Boy	Boy	Boy	Girl	Boy	Girl	Girl	Boy	Girl	Girl
27	Girl	Girl	Boy	Boy	Girl	Boy	Girl	Girl	Boy	Girl	Boy	Boy
28	Boy	Boy	Boy	Girl	Girl	Boy	Girl	Boy	Girl	Girl	Boy	Girl
29	Girl	Boy	Girl	Girl	Boy	Girl	Girl	Boy	Girl	Boy	Girl	Girl
30	Boy	Boy	Girl	Boy	Girl	Boy	Boy	Boy	Boy	Boy	Boy	Boy
31	Boy	Boy	Boy	Boy	Girl	Girl	Boy	Girl	Boy	Girl	Girl	Girl
32	Boy	Girl	Girl	Boy	Girl	Boy	Boy	Girl	Boy	Boy	Girl	Boy
33	Girl	Boy	Boy	Girl	Girl	Boy	Girl	Boy	Girl	Boy	Boy	Girl
34	Boy	Boy	Girl	Girl	Boy	Girl	Boy	Girl	Boy	Boy	Girl	Girl
35	Boy	Girl	Boy	Girl	Boy	Girl	Girl	Boy	Girl	Boy	Girl	Boy
36	Boy	Girl	Boy	Boy	Boy	Girl	Boy	Boy	Girl	Girl	Girl	Girl
37	Girl	Girl	Boy	Girl	Girl	Girl	Boy	Boy	Girl	Boy	Boy	Boy
38	Boy	Boy	Girl	Girl	Boy	Girl	Girl	Boy	Girl	Girl	Boy	Girl
39	Girl	Girl	Boy	Girl	Girl	Girl	Boy	Girl	Boy	Boy	Girl	Boy
40	Boy	Boy	Boy	Girl	Boy	Girl	Boy	Girl	Boy	Girl	Girl	Boy
41	Girl	Girl	Boy	Girl	Boy	Boy	Girl	Girl	Boy	Girl	Boy	Girl
42	Boy	Girl	Girl	Boy	Boy	Boy	Boy	Boy	Girl	Boy	Girl	Boy
43	Girl	Boy	Girl	Girl	Boy	Boy	Boy	Girl	Girl	Girl	Boy	Boy
44	Boy	Girl	Girl	Girl	Boy	Girl	Boy	Boy	Girl	Boy	Girl	Boy
45	Girl	Boy	Girl	Boy	Girl	Girl	Boy	Girl	Boy	Girl	Boy	Girl

- The numbers on the left of the Chinese Pregnancy Calendar indicate the mother's age at the time of conception.
- The months indicated at the top of the Chinese Pregnancy Calendar indicate when the baby was conceived.
- Follow the row across for the mother's age and follow the column down for the month the baby was conceived.
- The spot where the row and column meet will indicate the gender of the baby according to the Chinese Pregnancy Calendar.

For more information on the Chinese Pregnancy Calendar, see www.babynames.org.uk

Useful Contacts

Medical

Australian Action on Pre-eclampsia (AUS)

www.aapec.org.au

Tel: 03 9330 0441

Provides information about pre-eclampsia and support
for women suffering from it and their partners.

Australasian Diabetes in Pregnancy (AUS)

www.adips.org

Provides information about diabetes in pregnancy.

Australian Sports Commission (AUS)

www.ausport.gov.au/participating/women/resources/pregnancy

Provides information about playing sport while pregnant.

Multiple Birth Association of Australia (AUS)

www.amba.org.au

Tel: 1300 886 499

Provides information and support for those who are blessed
with twins or more!

NSW Department of Sport and Recreation (NSW)

www.dsr.nsw.gov.au/active/tips_pregnancy.asp

Tel: 13 13 02

Provides fitness advice and suggested activities
for the whole (new) family.

Pre-eclampsia Foundation (USA)

www.preeclampsia.org

Provides useful information about
pre-eclampsia.

Other Useful Contacts

Australian Government Child Care Access Hotline (AUS)
www.australia.gov.au/service/child-care-access-hotline
Tel: 1800 670 305
Provides information about access to childcare.

Australian Taxation Office (AUS)
www.ato.gov.au
Provides information concerning the tax implications of your
pregnancy and new baby.

Centrelink (AUS)
www.centrelink.gov.au
Provides information and advice on childcare benefit payments.

Child Care Benefit (AUS)
www.familyassist.gov.au/Internet/FAO/FAO1.nsf/content/
payments-ccb
Tel: 13 61 50
Child Care Benefit is a payment to help families who use
approved and registered childcare.

Fair Work Australia (AUS)
www.fwa.gov.au
Provides assistance and advice for unfair dismissal cases.

WageNet (AUS)
www.fairwork.gov.au
Provides information about wages and conditions
of employment in Australia for work that is
covered by federal awards and agreements.

**Read more: www.babycenter.com.au/
a-z/workingparents**

5

The Final Countdown
The Third Trimester Checklist

- ☑ Arrange for time to attend antenatal classes (they aren't cool, but you need 'em!).
- ☑ Practise smiling and looking interested in preparation for antenatal classes
- ☑ Get organised for B-day (or is it D-day?) by following our step-by-step guide.
- ☑ Make sure you or your partner has given notice to your employer at least 10 weeks prior to the birth.
- ☑ Sit down with your partner and write up a birth plan.
- ☑ Invite a few friends or family members to help during the labour, and explain to them your expectations for the birth.
- ☑ Get your house ready for the arrival of the baby, and help your partner pack a bag for hospital.
- ☑ Choose a name.
- ☑ Feel the baby kick.
- ☑ Wait for the fireworks!

In the third trimester everything can seem serene: your partner is beautifully pregnant, radiant with love and energy, and the baby is almost ready to pop out. All's well, right?

While everything seems calm, if you look carefully you'll see flashes of lightning on the horizon and hear the wind picking up in the trees.

The birth of your baby can only be successfully managed with sound preparation. Preparation protects you in the middle of the tempest, allowing you to emerge, post-event, intact in mind, body and spirit. Of course you've battened down the hatches at home, prepared the baby's space, got all the things you need for the foreseeable future for your baby and partner, but how do you prepare *mentally* for the big day?

Birth is not for the faint-hearted. The basic principle behind the psychology of surviving the delivery of your baby is to keep your composure at all times. To get through this experience unscathed, you need the mental agility of the tiger, the psychic strength of the ox and the stomach of an obese kid in a hot-dog-eating competition.

No matter the abuse you receive from your partner, no matter the sights you see, you'll need to reach inside and find your own little chill-out room. If you can smile and make pleasant conversation while your partner hurls abuse your way in the throes of labour, you'll know you're there.

In the meantime, whatever you do, don't get lulled into a false sense of security in the third trimester. You're experiencing the calm before the storm. Read the following step-by-step guide, and prepare yourselves …

Step 1: Get to Antenatal Classes

That's right, antenatal classes. Remember, 'ante' means before, and 'natal' means birth. So that's before-birth classes, or birth classes. Anyone?

These classes are without doubt very useful, primarily in terms of the information you will receive on what to do at the actual birth, but also in gaining solace from the fact that other people are experiencing exactly the same fears, trials and tribulations as you and your partner.

However, as you walk through the door of that room with its floor scattered with beanbags and its walls decorated with posters promoting breastfeeding and female-empowerment workshops, I'm sure you will think of 10 000 places you would rather be (the pub for one). However painful, all education has its uses, and admit it: you and your partner are both headed into uncharted waters.

Yes, being in a room full of pregnant women rabid with hormones can be a terrifying experience for all males involved. Add to this the fact that classes are usually held on a weeknight after a particularly hard day's work, and those sleep-inducing beanbags are obligatory (although probably meant for the females in the group, come to think of it). Furthermore, the classes are usually run by ever-so-bubbly peaches-and-cream-type midwives who turn into snarling Rottweilers if you ask dumb questions (which, let's face it, is in your nature).

As you squint through the fog of oestrogen at the chirpy instructor, keep the following do's and don'ts in mind:

DO:
- drink excessive amounts of coffee before going in;
- look like you are paying absolute attention to what is being said;
- make sure that any questions you ask are clear and concise and cannot be misinterpreted as even slightly offensive to pregnant women;
- take a seat at the back of the room (not in a beanbag, fool!) and stay upright and alert.

www.commons.wikimedia.org

The beanbag: scourge of antenatal classes.

A ship under sail and a big-bellied woman are the handsomest two things that can be seen common.

Benjamin Franklin

DON'T:
- drink excessive amounts of alcohol before going in (you can do that afterwards);
- fall asleep while watching a scintillating educational DVD, only to wake up to ask exactly those questions already answered in the aforementioned DVD;
- under any circumstances say anything that in any way could be interpreted as even vaguely sexist;
- make jokes or witty asides (no matter how blisteringly funny) about the content of the classes;
- at any stage say, 'Do you mind if we just skip to the birth bit?'

On a more serious note, antenatal classes will supply information on:
- what happens during labour and birth;
- what birthing options your partner has when she gives birth;
- coping with labour, and information about managing pain (hers, not yours);
- the role of the support person;
- exercises to keep your partner fit during pregnancy and to help her during labour;
- caring for the newborn;
- feeding options;
- emotions surrounding pregnancy, birth and the early postnatal period;
- the changes to your partner's body after the baby is born or;
- birth-control options postpartum.

Although passing around diaphragms or IUDs in front of a group of strangers is not everyone's idea of a great night out, antenatal classes can introduce you to what to expect as a support person and/or companion. You

If pregnancy were a book they would cut the last two chapters.
Nora Ephron

Love and pregnancy and riding on a camel cannot be hid.
Arabic proverb

can also meet some interesting people who are in the same situation as you. So suck it in, guys, and remember: knowledge is power!

Step 2: Develop a Birth Plan

So, you've been to antenatal classes and have a bit more of an idea about what's going on. Your partner, in addition to attending the classes with you, will have read about 250 books on pregnancy, so she probably has a pretty clear vision of how she wants the little tacker born. One way of harnessing her vision is by putting it down on paper. (If *you* suggest doing this, she's going to give you major brownie points.) So kick on back with a glass of sparkling water and get started on developing a birth plan.

A birth plan will help guide you both through labour and birth. Think of it like the instructions for flat-pack furniture: they may not always be necessary to do the job, but they'll help make erecting that home-entertainment unit a bit easier.

Sit down together and come up with a document that outlines how you want the labour and birth thing to go! Use it as a guide to prepare the stuff you're going to need, give a copy to your caregiver during an antenatal visit or when your partner is in labour and keep it with you during the whole labour and birth thing.

A birth plan has three purposes:
• it guides your caregiver(s) to help you have the birth experience you want. This is useful if you have a team of caregivers.
• it helps you get organised. If your partner desires Tibetan temple music in labour … you might go and buy some.
• if things feel like they are getting a little out of control in labour a birth plan can help you remember what is important for you both.

Following is a birth-plan question sheet you might like to copy or fill out. Please consult Chapters 6 and 7 for information to help you make decisions about some of the questions asked on it.

BIRTH PLAN

Support People

Who do you want present at the birth?

....

....

....

What do you want them to do?

....

....

....

Labour and Birth

How would you like to give birth?

....

....

....

....

What are your feelings about pain relief?

....

....

....

....

....

....

If you want pain relief, what sort would you like? If you want to try more
than one type of pain relief, in what order do you want to try them?

....

....

....

What do you want to happen to the baby when he/she is delivered?

....

....

....

Do you want to cut the umbilical cord?

....

....

....

Do you want to donate cord blood?

....

....

Do you have any thoughts about the delivery of the placenta or what you are going to do with it afterwards?

....

....

....

....

After the Birth

Oral versus injection of vitamin K for the bub – what is your preference?

....

....

....

Do you have any thoughts about feeding the baby?

....

....

....

Is there anything else you need?

....

....

....

....

....

....

....

Remember that labour and birth can be a bit of a roller-coaster ride and that things can change quickly, so it's a good idea not to be too attached to any particular part of your plan. Coming out at the other end with a healthy partner and child is usually more than enough for most people.

To Be (There) or Not To Be (There)

When you are working on your plan it may be a good idea to tell your partner if you're concerned about being present at the birth. Gone (some would say unfortunately!) are the days of bringing the little one into the world by getting drunk in a pub and smoking a couple of cigars with your mates.

No, nowadays it's pretty well expected that you will be present at your child's birth. But just how involved you want to be is up to you. For instance, you could agree to go along and stay at the 'top end' and do all the hand-holding and brow-wiping, while another support person attends to the areas you find uncomfortable.

The main thing is, if you are a bit squeamish, or extremely uncomfortable about it all, it's best to be up-front with your partner and talk about your concerns early on in the piece.

Who Let the Men In?

As you have probably gathered from your own dad's recollections, things were different not so long ago: 'You were an easy birth – I wasn't there.' Unless your parents were hippie types, pre-eighties dads pretty much paced around the waiting room before appearing to blow cigar smoke into the face of the newborn. That or they got sozzled at the local with a few mates for moral support, then went to see the fruits of their labour a few days later.

Yes, things have changed, but there was a time when it was actually a health hazard for a male to attend a birth, as Dr Wertt of Hamburg found out in 1522. An inquisitive soul, the aforementioned doctor dressed in women's clothes in order to get a better look at what happens in the (then) women's-only domain of childbirth. Unfortunately for Wertt, he didn't look that convincing in drag and was found out. The result? He was tried as a witch and summarily burned to death. Or so the story goes.

Step 3: Sort Out the Baby's 'Space'

Many women, like many animals, have a nesting instinct that picks up speed as the big day approaches. Instead of collecting twigs, however, women tend to collect more expensive things, like cutesy teddy bears, baby-blue curtains, strange talking mobiles (not phones, boofhead – those things that hang above the cot) and other inexplicable baby paraphernalia.

After arriving home to a totally redecorated house, you'll soon realise the nesting urge can be a force of nature and that in most cases it's often best to stand back (if you don't want to get hurt). Keep in mind, however, that in this bizarre state of elated energy your partner may not be thinking logically, so make sure that:

- she avoids paint fumes (they're not good for pregnant women, so you'd better pay someone, or do it yourself);
- she doesn't lift heavy things, which she is more than likely to try and do;
- she avoids toxic cleaning products, particularly in cramped spaces;
- she avoids using any credit cards that are already under stress.

Stuff to Get

Beware, the third trimester can be hard on your wallet! The following list comprises the things you really need to get ready for the arrival of your new bub:

- a cot with a well-fitting mattress and mattress protector (kids vomit, poo and pee heaps!);
- something to change the baby's nappy on (you don't have to buy a change table if you have something that's sturdy and of suitable height);
- something to wash the baby in, such as a baby bath (or the laundry/kitchen sink for tight-arses – but remember to take the dishes out first!);
- a nappy bucket with a tight-fitting lid (baby poo stinks!);
- a pram;
- a car baby capsule (these can he hired). Make sure this is fitted and ready to go before it's time to bring the little one home. Most areas have free safety checks of baby seats to ensure they are correctly fitted.

Make sure, guys, that whatever you buy meets the Australian Standards. For the health and safety of your new baby, it's important to ensure you are buying approved products.

The baby will also need:

- 6 singlets;
- 6 jumpsuits;
- 4 outfits;
- 2 cardigans;
- a jacket for winter;
- towels, washers and mild, non-scented soap;
- sheets and blankets;
- 36 nappies and a few plastic fasteners (if you are going cloth nappies), *or*
- 2 packets of disposable infant nappies (to start with, if you are going disposable nappies).

Step 4: Pack for the Hospital

Get the following stuff ready, well before your baby is due to arrive.

Your partner will need:

- a few nightdresses, or whatever she normally sleeps in;
- undies;
- a maternity bra for breastfeeding;
- sanitary pads;
- toiletries;
- a few comfortable clothes for the postnatal ward (ones that make it easy to pop those breasts out, if breastfeeding);
- some sort of entertainment (books, magazines, conkers, cards for strip-poker – your partner will be naked eventually, why not help out?)

Support people will need:

- some food;
- boardshorts (if you're doing some sort of water birth thing!);
- cameras and video stuff (fully charged, and with enough memory!).

The baby will need:

- nappies and fasteners;

- a beanie;
- clothes to wear on leaving the hospital;
- a blanket for departure.

And don't forget!!!

- cigars;
- champagne;
- fully charged batteries in your camera/video/phone.

Step 5: Plan the Route

It's a good idea to know the route from your place to the hospital for when the labour actually begins. You'll need to account for time of day, congestion, traffic lights, crosswinds and the distractions of your loudly moaning partner. You might even like to time a practice run (but remember, on the big day it's not the Daytona, lads: only one lap!).

Your Partner in the Third Trimester
Physical Changes in Your Loved One

In the third trimester your partner's body continues to grow and change. It's a terrifying but beautiful thing.

Breasts

The swelling of your partner's breasts may decrease towards the end of pregnancy, and they may spontaneously leak colostrum (the milk secreted just before, and for a short period after, giving birth). They are finally ready to become the food dispensers that nature intended. It is thought by some that nipple stimulation releases the wonder hormone oxytocin that can also start labour.

Uterus

By the end of the pregnancy your partner's abdomen is stretched to maximum capacity (I don't think she'll make it, Captain!). Every woman is different, but on average your dear one is carrying an extra 11.6 kilograms, most of that being situated in her abdomen.

You can actually break it down by the kilogram: baby 3.2 kilograms, placenta 0.6 kilogram, amniotic fluid 0.8 kilogram, breasts 0.4 kilogram (cool!), blood 1.5 kilograms, water 2.6 kilograms and extra fat 2.5 kilograms (but don't tell her that!).

Coming Out in Sympathy

Of interest to the flabbier among us will be a study by British research company Onepoll in 2009, which announced that the average weight gain during pregnancy was just over 6 kilograms … and that was for our British *bros*!

Of the 5000 geezers surveyed, the reasons for eating more while their partners were pregnant were many and varied. The biggest blame went on eating out more frequently before the baby was due, and on the increased availability of snacks in the house. Being served larger portions by hungrier mums was another supposed factor, while a quarter of those surveyed claimed their overeating was related to a desire to make their partners feel better about their own weight gain. (Yeah right, gutso!)

There is actually evidence that some men *do* experience the symptoms of their pregnant partners, in what has been termed couvade syndrome, from the French word *couver*, meaning 'to hatch'. In 2007, researchers at the University of London monitored 282 fathers-to-be aged between 19 and 55, and compared them to a control group.

The destined-dads group experienced a range of pregnancy-like symptoms which included anything from cramps

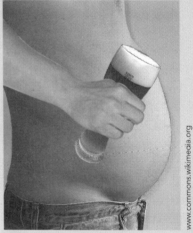

www.commons.wikimedia.org

and back pain to food cravings and mood swings. Some men actually got larger bellies, or 'baby-bumps'. In 11 of the cases, men went to see doctors about their symptoms, but no diagnosis for their complaints could be found. It seems the majority of the symptoms faded in the early stages of their partner's pregnancy, but for a few the complaints lasted right up until the baby was delivered.

The convener of the study, Dr Arthur Brennan, stated that the symptoms were definitely involuntary. Although there was some speculation as to the role of hormones and possible psychological causes, no definitive explanation could be found for the symptoms.

So if you're a bit flabby, use it for an excuse while the jury is still out.

Heart
Your good partner's heart has done a great job. It has managed to deal with the extra beating and blood volume supplying your little one with all the oxygen and nutrients it needs. Towards the end of pregnancy your partner's heart is moving an extra three litres of blood and is working 40 per cent harder than the heart of a non-pregnant woman.

Hormones
Oxytocin is the love drug. While it's best known for its role in female reproduction, this hormone is also thought to have a role in social recognition, anxiety, trust, orgasm, maternal behaviour and, of course, love.

In pregnancy, oxytocin is responsible for contracting the uterus in labour and allowing milk to be released from the milk ducts where it's stored. Oxytocin also aids in stopping bleeding and allowing the uterus to shrink following birth.

Things That Might Piss Your Partner Off

Heartburn
This has nothing to do with your partner's heart, so rest easy. Gastric juices (containing acid) travel up the oesophagus and cause a horrid burning sensation.

Heartburn is common, affecting about two-thirds of all women at some stage during pregnancy. It is thought to be caused by the muscles relaxing as a result of hormones and, later in pregnancy, by increased pressure in the abdomen. Many women complain of heartburn after stooping or lying down.

You may want to think about purchasing shares in Mylanta. Other relief measures for your partner are to sleep with extra pillows under her head and shoulders, and to avoid fatty or spicy foods. Some medications can help, but see your caregiver first.

Fainting
Fainting can be caused by a momentary lack of blood to the brain. Some scientific folk believe that fainting is one of our most ancient of reflexes. (Indeed, you can find examples of fainting practised expertly by women throughout time, usually when shocked by the sight of nudity or when faced with some kind of

What Baby?

Your partner can't find the keys, has forgotten her doctor's appointment and is generally a bit vague. Anecdotal evidence strongly suggests that pregnant women may suffer some form of short-term memory loss, or 'Baby Brain', as it is sometimes nicknamed, particularly in the third trimester. As far as hard evidence goes, however, studies into the phenomenon are conflicting.

One study suggests that memory loss in pregnant women may be more related to self-idealisation. The study interviewed 15 pregnant women about their memory and found that the group felt strongly that their memory was worse than it was before they were pregnant.

The pregnant women were then given two memory tests, one at six months pregnant and one a year after birth, in conjunction with a non-pregnant group of women. The results were that the pregnant women performed no worse than the non-pregnant women, leading researchers to believe that much of reported memory loss in pregnancy may be perceived rather than actual.

Other studies, however, report the opposite. A 1998 study published in the *American Journal of Obstetrics and Gynecology* showed a 15 per cent deficit in the short-term memory of women in their third trimester compared to the rest of the population.

More research reported in the *American Journal of Psychosomatic Obstetrics* found a significant decrease in the memory of pregnant women and a relationship between anxiety levels and loss of memory. 'Anxiety' related to the overload of information that women have to absorb when birth is imminent. Factors such as fear of the unknown and the responsibility of bringing up a child were cited as major distractions in clouding memory.

The general assumption is that a combination of stress, exhaustion, fear of the unknown and having a lot of things happening can affect your other-half's memory ... but you probably don't need a team of scientists to tell you that.

moral complexity. Countless books, and a great many black-and-white films, have faithfully recorded this for us.)

In pregnancy, women usually faint as a result of progesterone dilating the blood vessels, which results in a lowering of blood pressure and therefore a disruption to the supply of blood to the brain. It can also happen when lying down directly on her back – the big lump of a child she is carrying inside her can press onto her major blood vessels, restricting the flow of blood. Your partner should therefore only lie on her side.

While fainting is not normally harmful in itself, falling and hitting objects on the way down usually is.

If your partner feels dizzy, sees spots in front of her eyes, or feels suddenly like crap the best thing she can do is:
• ask for help;
• lower herself to a chair or onto the ground;
• wait for the dizzy feeling to pass and slowly get up;
• after the event … tell someone about it.

Be aware that fainting may also be a symptom of a more serious problem, so if a fainting episode does occur, get your partner checked out.

Haemorrhoids
Haemorrhoids are inflamed or clotted veins (inside or outside the bum) and are commonly known as piles. What can you say about haemorrhoids? They are painful, unpleasant and, due to the presence of the hormone progesterone, your pregnant partner is more likely to get them than not. The best thing to do is get some medicine from the pharmacy to help treat them. Some research suggests haemorrhoids can be effectively managed when constipation is successfully controlled. See 'Constipation', below (no pun intended!).

Constipation
It is common that our pregnant ones will become constipated at some stage in their pregnancy. To treat, increase fruit, vegetable and drink intake. Laxatives can help, but get your partner to see her caregiver first.

Leg Swelling
There is a lot of extra fluid sloshing around inside your partner, and some of this will pool in the feet and ankles, causing a swollen appearance and a feeling of heaviness. A little bit of extra fluid around the ankles is normal, but if your partner is swelling up like a water balloon, you should get it checked out.

For minor swelling, some women report relief with a warm bath, and/or by putting her feet up while sitting, and/or by calf massage (get to it, guys!). The wearing of attractive support stockings – bought from the chemist's or obtained through your caregiver – can also assist in keeping the fluid at bay.

Carpal Tunnel Syndrome
In later pregnancy swelling in the hands and wrists can press on the nerves and cause numbness and pain. This is known as carpal tunnel syndrome and can be very distressing for your long-suffering partner. Thankfully there are a couple of simple things she can do to alleviate her suffering:
• rest her elbow on a pillow and elevate her hand, this might reduce the swelling;
• regularly flex her fingers and wrist.

Hand numbness can also be a symptom of some serious medical problems like stroke and should be checked out promptly. Also, if your partner is unable to deal with the pain she should see her caregiver and other treatment, like physiotherapy, can be organised.

Varicose Veins
These are the swollen leg veins normally seen on your nanna. Symptoms include pain in the legs. (Obvious.) Wear support stockings for relief.

Some poor women can get varicose veins in the vulva or the vagina. They should see their caregiver for treatment advice.

Braxton Hicks Contractions
These are irregular and generally painless contractions thought to improve blood flow to the placenta and bub. However, they should be checked out if they become very painful or regular.

Naming the Baby
It'll most likely be in this trimester that you start to get serious about your child's name. There is a lot of advice out there for naming babies – most of which, quite frankly, is bleedingly obvious. For example:
The name should have a positive connotation for you.
Sound advice if you were thinking of the name Stalin or Hitler.

Is the name easy to spell?

If you name your baby 'Sarah', spelt S-Z-A-R-R-A-A-H, it's got to be pretty obvious that she'll be spelling out her name and cursing her parents for the rest of her living days.

Is it easy to remember?

Ummm, is what easy to remember?

Do the initials form a word? If so, is that word likely to prove embarrassing in any way?

Like R. Sole? Point taken!

Celebrity Names

Everybody knows that celebrity actors and musicians want nothing more than to be left alone to practise their art without journalists ruthlessly splashing their lives across the tabloid media and so-called 'glossies'. So why, then, do they come up with such attention-grabbing names for their fledgling offspring?

Gwyneth Paltrow and Chris Martin chose Apple for their daughter's name, not in reference to the latest Hollywood diet but because 'Apples are so sweet, and they're wholesome, and it's biblical and I just thought it sounded so lovely and clean', as Gwyneth told Oprah in an interview in 2004.

David and Victoria Beckham obviously hoped the ugly gene wouldn't conspire against them, calling their son Romeo, while Brangelina must have betted that spoonerisms or rhyming slang would never be used to create nicknames at their daughter's future exclusive school: Shiloh Pitt, ummm? – Pile of ...

Shiloh and Apple, as it happens, are abnormally normal when compared to other celebrity bub names on offer, particularly in the US. Comedian Penn Jillette chose the name Moxie CrimeFighter for his daughter, while Jason Lee of *My Name is Earl* fame cooked up Pilot Inspektor.

While all these names will possibly leave celeb sprogs hoping it's possible to change not their names but their *parents* by deed poll, they'll at least have the consolation of being able to easily find a Gmail address. And they can take comfort in the fact that attention-grabbing names are not a new phenomenon. Flash back to sixties experimental rocker Frank Zappa, who is quoted as saying that his job was 'extrapolating everything to its most absurd extreme', a philosophy he obviously applied to naming his kids, Moon Unit, Dweezil, Ahmet and Diva Muffin.

On a more serious note, one thing to think about, which you may have forgotten, is the fact that you might want to honour a relative or friend with the middle name, or first name if you really want to pay homage. Beyond this, Australian laws about naming a baby try to prevent some other interesting baby-naming ideas:

- you cannot choose a name which includes an official title or rank, like 'Prince Michael' or 'The Captain'.
- you cannot choose a name which is a trademark, for example 'Woolworths' or 'British Petroleum'.

What's in a Name?

Ever wondered why some names suddenly become popular, while others inexplicably go the way of Sheila and Darren? Steven D. Levitt and Stephen J. Dubner may have the answer for you, as their bestselling book *Freakonomics* examines exactly this question. The answer seems to be class.

Freakonomics crunched the numbers on the Californian birth-certificate database, which stretches back to 1961. The data, which includes more than 16 million documents, contains standard information including: name, gender, race, birth weight and marital status. More revealing, however, are the socio-economic indicators, such as zip codes, parental education and the method of paying the hospital bill, which are also present in the data.

Using statistical analysis, the authors concluded that names, over a relatively short period of time, move down through socio-economic sub-strata before becoming extinct.

The Californian data showed that those names that are popular with highly educated, and presumably richer, parents quickly move to the middle classes, and then on to low-earning families. By the time they have gained popularity with the working classes, these names are out of fashion with the top end of town and relegated to eventual extinction, and so the cycle starts again.

The authors' conclusions on these discoveries are that parents find names for their children, on a subconscious level, from those with bigger mortgages and more financial freedom. A parent's choice of name, it seems, is a signal of their own expectations as to how they hope their child will turn out.

So what's wrong with Sheila and Dazza, anyway?

Kiwi Name Issues

As reported in the New Zealand *Herald* in 2008, New Plymouth magistrate Rob Murfitt allowed a nine-year-old girl named (wait for it) Talula Does The Hula From Hawaii to become a ward of the state in order to change her name by deed poll.

Judge Murfitt reasoned that the name embarrassed the youth and exposed her to teasing and possible bullying, therefore giving her the right to override her parents' choice of name.

The ruling exposed what seems to be a reasonably common problem in New Zealand, with the judge citing other examples of names which had been blocked by courts. Some of the weirder ones included Twisty Poi, Sex Fruit, Got Lucy and Yeah Detroit. Strangely, others, such as Number 16 Bus Shelter, Violence, Midnight Chardonnay and unfortunate twins Benson and Hedges had passed muster and previously been allowed.

Another case also emerged of a girl being named in text-speak as O.crnia. In this case the mother conceded to the court's order to rename the child Oceania. Judge Murfitt stated that the bizarre names mentioned amounted to a 'social handicap' for those lumbered with them, and encouraged parents to think hard before naming their children.

Ah yes, our poor Kiwi cousins … That could never happen here, could it?

Well before we get too smug, Gummy Bear, Coca Cola and King John 1 are just three names rejected by Australia's Registry of Births, Deaths and Marriages in 2008.

- you cannot choose a name which consists of or includes symbols without phonetic significance, for example '%' or '@'. (F#*%, lucky they put that bit in!)

One last thing to take into account is it's also best to keep in mind short and succinct names that are easy to yell. Long names, say something like 'Ebenezer' don't really roll off the tongue, especially in sentences like, 'Ebenezer, put that chainsaw down!' or, 'Ernestina, your grandfather's head is not a monkey bar!'

Nicknames stick to people, and the most ridiculous are the most adhesive.

Thomas C. Haliburton

Your Baby in the Third Trimester

28–32 weeks	By 32 weeks your baby weighs about 2100 grams and is approximately 30 centimetres long (measured crown to rump). If your little one sports a Y chromosome somewhere in its genetic make-up, around the 28-week mark his testicles will descend into his scrotum. Lanugo, that weird pre-birth hair, disappears from your baby's face and its skin starts to lose its red appearance.
32–36 weeks	By the 36th week the baby will have piled on the pork and be a hefty 2900 grams and 34 centimetres long. The lanugo now disappears entirely from the body, and hair starts to grow on the little tacker's head (this could be the beginning of your child's very first bad hair day!). Ready for a life of crime, your baby's hand print is now complete with the appearance of the palm crease.
36–40 weeks	At approximately 3400 grams and 36 centimetres at 38 weeks, your baby is big enough to face the outside world. The timer has gone off on the oven: it's time for the big bang! Your baby's skull, which is made up of multiple plates, starts to firm, and the head may 'engage', or move down into your partner's pelvis as it lines up for the almighty squeeze down the birth canal and the great escape from the womb.

Medical Stuff in the Third Trimester

Your partner will be glad to know that most of the testing has been sorted in the first and second trimesters. In the third trimester, regular antenatal visits continue but the schedule of visits increases as B-day approaches. It's the same old stuff: weight taking, wee testing, belly measuring, listening to the baby's heartbeat. The following timetable sets it all out.

Care Timetable

27–36 weeks	Review by an obstetrician (if you are being looked after by one), plus fortnightly visits by caregiver Anti-D injection (if required) (see Chapter 4) Blood tests such as a blood group test and full blood count (see Chapter 3) are generally repeated Vaginal swab
37–40 weeks	Weekly review by caregiver
41 + weeks	Your partner is now officially overdue and needs a review by your caregiver/obstetrician to decide on a plan of action (see 'Overdue … What Do We Do?', pages 134–138)

Possible Serious Stuff to Worry About

Look guys, your partner is in the third trimester. She is almost ready to give birth but unfortunately there are still some big speed humps you might need to negotiate before you cross the finish line.

Pre-term Rupture of the Membranes

This is a fancy description for early breaking of the waters. If your partner has complained about unexplained leaking of fluid from her vagina, she may have ruptured her waters. In this case you'd best get her to your caregiver for assessment, quick smart.

Early ruptures are caused when the membranes which hold the amniotic fluid break before the start of labour. There are two main risks attached to this: infection, and pre-term labour (see 'Pre-term Labour', pages 132–133).

If labour doesn't follow rupture, a serious discussion with your caregiver needs to take place concerning risks to the baby due to early birth versus risks from infection.

Hospitalisation will probably be necessary, with the administration of antibiotics or the possible induction of labour.

Breech Presentation

As your partner can no doubt tell you your baby spends a great deal of time flipping and moving around the uterus and can even spend some of its time upside-down. However, around 36 weeks it gets so tight a squeeze in there that the upside-down baby can't turn back. They are stuck. If your partner goes into labour the baby will be born bum first.

As you probably already know, most babies come out head first, but some babies want to come out bum or leg first, and this is called 'being in breech'.

This may seem insignificant, but it can cause some serious problems to the baby while it is being delivered. A few years ago a large and internationally recognised clinical trial showed that breech birth is much more dangerous than a head-first delivery and consequently should be avoided in the interest of the baby's safety. There are, however, some professionals who disagree with these conclusions, believing that with appropriate training and experience breech delivery is as safe as head-first delivery.

If your baby is the wrong way round, there are a couple of treatment options.

The first is a specialised manoeuvre called external cephalic version, wherein a specially trained caregiver (an obstetrician) flips the baby over by applying force on your partner's abdomen, hopefully resulting in the baby's head facing the right direction for a vaginal birth. This is usually identified by your caregiver feeling your partner's abdomen during a routine antenatal visit. Breech is confirmed by ultrasound. It is done from 36 weeks. It should not be painful for your partner and feels mighty strange when the baby flips.

Monitoring of both your partner and baby by CTG (cardiotocograph, see page 156) is necessary to observe for potential complications. This procedure is not always successful.

If the stubborn little bugger stays breech, a decision may be made to deliver it by caesarean section (see page 168).

Pre-term Labour

This is defined as the onset of labour before 37 weeks. Regular contractions before 37 weeks must be investigated as a matter of urgency.

Contractions may stop (either spontaneously or with the help of drugs) or may lead to established labour and birth. If the labour can't be stopped, this can be a serious problem. Premature babies aren't well adapted for life outside the womb. The earlier a baby is born, the poorer are its prospects of survival and the greater is its risk of having a permanent disability. The immaturity of a premature baby's lungs is usually of primary concern.

After initial assessment and treatment for pre-term labour, your partner may be moved to a hospital with a neonatal intensive care unit to give your baby the best chance (see 'Having a Baby in a Neonatal Intensive Care Unit', page 172).

Some of the causes of pre-term labour include:
• premature rupture of the membranes;
• smoking, and other lifestyle issues;
• being an older, or a very young, mother;
• problems with the cervix;
• infection.

Relaxation for Labour

Relaxation is a great lifelong skill to learn; everyone can benefit from it. In labour, relaxation can be useful in reducing the time it takes for your partner to push the little one out.

The theory behind this is a bit complicated but goes something like this. In times of stress, the body produces adrenaline, the 'fight or flight' drug. In turn, adrenaline suppresses the release of oxytocin, the hormone responsible for uterine contractions. It is therefore thought that increased stress equals decreased contractions, which equals a slower labour ... which, if you think about it, makes sense.

However, relaxation needs to be *practised* to be effective, so as a partner you ought to provide encouragement and time for your partner to relax. If she doesn't have a relaxation technique of her own, she might like to try the following in the months before the birth.

Get into a quiet environment. Get into a comfortable reclining position. (Shoes off, reggae on.) Try and concentrate on your breath entering through your mouth or nose. Exhale, and let all your muscles relax. Put your hands on your abdomen and feel it rise and fall while you continue to take breaths. Close your eyes and *relax* ...

If your partner goes into pre-term labour, she may be given drugs to (hopefully) stop labour, and she will most likely be given a steroid injection to help the baby's lungs to mature.

Placenta Praevia

The placenta that has been working to serve and protect your baby can sometimes stuff things up. One of the problems it can cause is a condition called placenta praevia, which is when the placenta grows (either fully or partially) over the cervix. This can cause serious problems if undetected, as the placenta can block the escape route to the outside world. During labour, as the baby is forced out it will damage the placenta, causing serious bleeding. This can be of consequence to both mother and child.

Fortunately, in the Western world most placenta praevia is identified during the 20-week morphology ultrasound. However, every now and then one will be missed and you can have problems. One of the signs of placenta praevia is unexplained, painless vaginal bleeding. Needless to say, this needs to be urgently checked out.

If your partner has been diagnosed with placenta praevia, it's important that you tell each new caregiver before any vaginal examination is undertaken. Birth by caesarean section may be recommended.

Cholestasis

If your loved one becomes terribly itchy in the second half of pregnancy, there is a chance she has developed cholestasis. This is caused by a problem with your partner's ability to break down the bile salts used in digestion. With cholestasis there is an increased risk of liver problems for the mother, and stillbirth for the baby … so extreme itchiness needs to be checked out by your caregiver or your local hospital. Hospitalisation and medication will be required.

No Foetal Movement

If your partner thinks that the baby is not moving, get to your local hospital. Chances are it won't be a problem – it's difficult to feel every hit, punch and kick when you live a busy life! But it's better to be on the safe side.

Overdue … What Do We Do?

You would expect your child to be fashionably late to future dinner engagements, exams and possibly to a wedding or two, but being late to his/her birth is very poor form. You and your partner have made plans and organised leave. Further to this, just about everyone who's important in your lives is waiting for that baby to come out … but there is a total no show!

Medically speaking, is this a problem?

Being overdue (which is defined as pregnancy that lasts 41 or more weeks) has been associated with an increase in illness and stillbirth for babies. It can also result in more difficult deliveries, as babies left to cook for too long tend to be on the larger side. This, obviously, doesn't make things so comfortable for labouring mothers. For these reasons, caregivers generally encourage the induction of labour.

Induction is the process of artificially making your partner go into labour. At the end of term, your partner (and hopefully you) will meet with your caregiver to discuss what options there are to bring this recalcitrant child into the world. Medical science still doesn't understand what triggers the labour process, but, through trial and error, has found that some things will get things moving along.

Induction of labour is not without risks (for your partner and baby), so you both need to discuss the risks versus the benefits with your caregiver. Here is a description of some of the techniques that may be recommended.

Sweep and Stretch
Your caregiver will do a vaginal examination and will manually stretch the cervix a little to separate the bottom of the membranes from the top of the cervix. This procedure may be slightly painful for your loved one, but evidence suggests that it is effective in bringing on labour. It has been shown to be safe unless your partner has placenta praevia.

Rupture of the Membranes
This is where your caregiver uses a blunt plastic hook to rupture the membranes. Breaking the waters will usually start labour, but it's not a sure-fire thing. One complication is that it may lead to infection. It may also be painful for your partner.

If the breaking of the waters is unsuccessful, most caregivers will commence your partner on an intravenous infusion of oxytocin.

Drugs To Bring On Labour
Clever people have come up with a range of drugs that will bring on labour. These drugs have been shown to work, but are not without risk. Some may restrict your partner to bed for labouring.

1. Prostaglandin
Prostaglandins are naturally occurring hormones that have been shown to 'ripen' (to become soft and stretchy) the cervix. In order to bring on labour, a prostaglandin gel is applied near the cervix.

Bring It On At Home

These methods of getting your baby out of the womb have been passed down from mother to daughter from the time when sex was invented. Although not scientifically tested, you may consider them worth a go!

The Hot Sex Theory

Sex is thought to bring on labour, and what's more it's free and lots of fun. The theory goes that:
1) the female orgasm may kick-start the process (no pressure, guys!);
2) oxytocin is released through intercourse, which may help move things along;
3) your semen contains prostaglandin, which is thought to help the cervix dilate.

NOTE: Sex should be safe unless your partner's waters have broken, unless she has placenta praevia or unless she has been advised against it by your caregiver.

The Hot Curry Theory

Wise women throughout time have thought that spicy food stimulates the gut, which pushes on the uterus, thus triggering labour. So give the hot curry theory a shot (unless your partner suffers heartburn).

If you are challenged in the kitchen, here is a recipe to help bring it on:

Your loved one and baby will be monitored to see if labour comes on or if there are any complications. If one dose is ineffective, another is applied.

A risk associated with the use of prostaglandins is hypertonic uterus. This is where the contractions become too strong or too frequent, which may restrict oxygen getting to the baby.

2. Oxytocin

Syntocinon, a synthetic version of oxytocin, is infused via an intravenous drip into your partner, inducing contractions. This will work, but anecdotally some women complain that it is a wild ride (like going from 0 to 100 km/h in an instant!). Because your partner will have an infusion via a drip, one disadvantage to this procedure is that she won't be able to birth in a bath, or walk around in labour.

Syntocinon is a very safe drug, but it may cause hypertonic uterus, plus some other very rare but serious issues like water

Red Lentil Curry Labour Soup

a dash of olive oil
2 small carrots, diced
1 large onion, finely chopped
4 stalks celery, sliced
3–4 cloves of garlic, crushed
2–3 tablespoons red curry paste
2 cups dried red lentils
4–5 cups finely diced potatoes
1–2 beef stock cubes
a sprinkle of ground cloves
  or cinnamon
salt and pepper, to taste

Heat the oil in a large soup pot over medium–high heat and add the carrot, onion, celery and garlic. Sauté for 10 minutes, then add the curry paste, lentils, potato, stock cubes and cloves or cinnamon. Cover with water, put on the lid and reduce heat to medium. Cook for about 1 hour, or until the potatoes and lentils are cooked. Season to taste with salt and pepper.

Serve topped with plain yoghurt and a garnish of chopped shallots. Enjoy with crusty white bread.

The Walking Theory

The wise women of yore have often touted walking as a method of triggering labour. It is thought that walking causes the bub's head to stimulate the cervix, releasing oxytocin and thus providing the spark for labour. A great excuse to sit watching sport on Sunday while your partner walks to get the Sunday papers. Or maybe not …

toxicity and uterine rupture. Also, babies born with the aid of this drug have an increased risk of jaundice (see Chapter 7).

Other Methods

There are some methods to bring on labour that haven't been fully explored by medical science but they are thought by some to be the spark that can start the fires of labour.

Acupuncture

Skilful practitioners using ancient knowledge and sharp little needles stimulate invisible meridians to trigger the labour process. There hasn't been a scientifically recognised trial that has proved the effectiveness of acupuncture, or its safety, but anecdotally many couples claim it is very effective.

Breast Stimulation

The hormone oxytocin that contracts the uterus is believed by some to be released due to breast stimulation. It is thought that if your partner's nipples are tweaked enough, the released hormone will trigger labour. Once again, this method has not been scientifically explored, and some folk think it can lead to a hypertonic uterus (see 'Prostaglandin', pages 135–136), so handle with care.

Movin' On …

B-day is approaching fast; it's nearly over. One more thing to do is to study up the next chapter. For, as Baden-Powell (leader of those kids wearing embarrassing green uniforms in public) always said: 'Be prepared!'

Useful Contacts

The National Premmie Foundation (AUS)
ww.prembaby.org.au
Tel: 1300 773 622
Provides contacts, information and support for parents with a premature baby.

Baby Names (AUS)
www.babynames.com.au
You guessed it, this site is a must-stop for all those undecided namers-to-be out there.

6

Babies, Blood and Cigars
Labour and Birth Checklist

☑ Read this chapter *before* the birth!

☑ If your partner is getting regular contractions, ring your caregiver and your support people.

☑ Offer your partner whatever support and pain relief you can while at home.

☑ Get everything you need for the hospital and put it in the car. If you forget the camera, you're a dead man.

☑ When your caregiver gives you the green light to head for the hospital, do so promptly but without haste – no running the red lights, guys!

☑ Hand over your birth plan at the hospital, but be ready to make changes to it if necessary.

☑ If pain relief or obstetric interventions are recommended by your caregiver, help your partner make sensible decisions about these things.

☑ Continue to offer support and encouragement through transition, the second stage of labour and all that comes after delivery.

☑ If you want the placenta for any reason (see 'What to Do With the Placenta', page 206), let your caregiver know.

☑ Get ready for shock and awe (or is it *arwgh*!?).

Watching, sorry helping, your partner give birth can be quite a confronting experience, partly as the first time round you're not going to have seen her, or anyone for that matter, going through the pain of labour. To get an idea of what it's going to be like (for your partner) imagine the groans and facial expressions of a WWE Wrestler, and now imagine they're not faking. Don't worry; it's all perfectly normal, unless a caregiver tells you otherwise.

Like bungee-jumping, you will experience terror along with overwhelming emotions, the difference being that bungee-jumping, once over, doesn't usually reduce a grown man to tears of joy. But have no doubt about it, of all those memorable events you go through in life – be it getting your first car, meeting your partner, getting married – you will remember your child's birth more clearly than any of them. Hell, you'll probably even be able to say the date and time two weeks down the track!

Although you and your partner are probably having major apprehensions about what you are about to go through, keep in mind, at the time of writing the world population was six billion, six hundred and ninety-seven million, two hundred and fifty-four thousand and forty-one. So what? I hear you ask, well this means that 13 394 508 082 parents, give or take a few, have successfully got through childbirth.

The other thing to keep in mind is that if you end up having a long-haul birth, at the end of the day (or, God forbid, *days*) when your little one pops out you won't remember any of the bad stuff.

It is a truly beautiful thing.

What is Labour and How Do I Know My Partner Is In Labour?

If you are reading this for the first time and your partner is in the next room screaming, God help you!

If not, then let's break this down. Labour involves heavy work by your partner's uterus and cervix, and a whole heap of pushing, resulting in a baby. Medical folk have divided the process of labour into three stages.

The first stage involves the opening of the cervix, the second stage is the pushing of the baby through the cervix and out of the vagina, and the third stage is the expulsion of the placenta. This chapter will explore these three stages in more detail.

While there is debate about what triggers labour, there is no debate about when labour starts. Labour starts when your partner is getting contractions that are:

- regular;
- getting stronger;
- coming more frequently;
- lasting longer.

If all these things are happening, to be clear, YOUR PARTNER IS IN LABOUR.

As you have no doubt heard, contractions are painful, so why are they necessary?

Simply put, a contraction is when the uterus starts to squeeze. The wonder organ that has housed your child throughout the pregnancy is basically a strong tube of muscle. For your baby to be born, the uterus must squeeze open the muscular gate at its end, otherwise known as the cervix, and press the baby through a hole in the pelvis, down the birth canal and out into the open air. This whole process is only possible with strong and effective contractions.

The Pain of Labour

Pain and childbirth go together like beers at the pub and a late-night kebab. Vaginal births hurt at the time, while caesarean sections hurt afterwards. The whole thing is like nothing you will ever experience. Lucky for you, you only have to witness it, not actually feel it.

You are about to watch your partner undergo

Giving birth is like taking your lower lip and forcing it over your head.
Carol Burnett

The 880-yard heel and toe walk is the closest a man can come to experiencing the pangs of childbirth.
Avery Brundage

A History of Childbirth

For those of you who pine for the good old days, when things were simpler and a little less busy, think of two modern medical marvels: dentistry and childbirth. If a bottle of hard spirits and a pair of pliers isn't enough to make you thank God that those times have changed, then childbirth definitely will.

Evidence points to the fact that, in primitive times, birthing was done outside the dwelling (so as not to mess up the cave floor) in the forest or by a stream, with a female friend or family member to help. Suffice to say, any complications were nearly always fatal.

The Romans, not content with creating the Olympics and conquering the Western world, were actually also skilled obstetricians. A guy called Soranus (AD 98–138) wrote a detailed textbook to aid in delivery, which included the first advice on the use of an obstetric chair. Soranus's handy tips for infant care included 'boiled water and honey for the child for the first two days, then on to the mother's breast.' Or words to that effect.

As the world slid into the Dark Ages, however, things became a little less refined, with birth and labour becoming a very risky venture for mother and child. Small pelvises or obstructed labour were the catalysts to uncountable deaths. Some believed that whipping the pregnant woman was the best way to induce labour. A medieval German empress (and early feminist) turned this technique on its head by supposedly having 20 men whipped in her labour room. Two of them reportedly died before she successfully gave birth.

the physical equivalent of ten rounds in the ring with Mike Tyson, so it is important to try to understand what she is going through and learn ways in which you can help.

So let's start this conversation off with a little bit of theory. Let's begin by asking, what is pain?

Pain has evolved as a complex defence mechanism to protect us against a dangerous world that seeks to eat, damage or injure us in thousands of ways. In response, the body has developed a complex nervous system that recognises bodily injury and sends messages to the brain. The brain then interprets these messages and stores away information about which experiences are dangerous and should be avoided in the future.

Perhaps the most disturbing aspect of medieval birth was the fact that simple lack of hygiene caused a multitude of deaths to mothers, newborns and, in some cases, the physicians themselves.

Puerperal fever, caused by an infection in the genital tract and often leading to septicaemia, reached epidemic proportions in 1772 with an estimated 20 per cent of all mothers in Paris, Vienna and other European capitals contracting the disease after labour. Two men, Alexander Gordon and Oliver Wendell Holmes, noticed that something was amiss with delivery practices. In 1795 Gordon suggested that puerperal fever was an infectious process, while later in 1843 Holmes published the controversial *The Contagiousness of Puerperal Fever*. The paper made the assumption that the fever was spread by doctors and nurses and suggested that clean clothing and avoidance of autopsies by those aiding birth would prevent the spread of puerperal fever. The paper was rejected by many with one of Holmes' associates, Charles Delucena Meigs, said to claim, 'Doctors are gentlemen, and gentlemen's hands are clean'.

In 1849 Ignaz Semmelweis (see 'Dr Ignaz Semmelweis, Saviour of Women', page 37), ignorant of Gordon and Holmes' discoveries, finally twigged, when an associate died of (presumed) septicaemia caused by a dissection wound. Semmelweis proved that puerperal fever could be eliminated through sanitary techniques in the hospital he managed. These sanitary techniques included wearing clean clothes and thoroughly scrubbing hands before aiding in delivery, facts that seem blatantly obvious to us in these modern times.

Unfortunately in labour there is no running; your partner must deal with it head-on. How an individual copes with pain depends on a variety of factors. The emotional state and energy levels of a labouring woman are particularly important when attempting to interpret and cope with childbirth.

Contraction pain starts much like mild backache or abdominal cramping and gets more intense as labour progresses. Over time the pain can seem unrelenting to a woman in labour, and with no end in sight a woman's morale can plummet, along with her ability to endure the pain of contractions.

Fortunately, as an antidote to all this, you will be there like a knight in shining armour to provide the support she needs.

In order to succeed in this role there are two main things you ought to do. Firstly, keep things relaxed by staying with her and providing encouragement. She needs to keep her eye on the prize and be reassured that she can get there. Secondly, keep her well supplied with food and water. Running on empty can be associated with a corresponding fall in morale and reduced ability to cope with pain. (Note, however, that sometimes restrictions are put on the consumption of food and drink with caesarean births. Check with your caregiver.)

The Role of Support People

Most men in Australia will be support people for their partners during labour and birth. From the dawn of time, support people have braved the impossible while witnessing the miraculous. As a support person you will have a major role in the labour and birth process, so it's worthwhile looking at the job description.

Labour Assistant If your partner wants a shoulder to lean on, it's expected that you provide it. You may find yourself being a human Hill's Hoist, providing essential upright support to your labouring partner.

Liaison Officer During labour and birth your partner might not be in the best psychological state to communicate with others, and her vocabulary is likely to consist of grunts, groans and the occasional obscenity. You, therefore, may have to assist her by acting as an interpreter in communications with your caregivers.

Team Psychologist and Motivational Therapist Labour can be a roller-coaster ride of emotions, with your partner moving between excitement and despair. Your role is to try and keep her on as even a keel as possible in order to get her through labour. Good luck, buddy!

Decision-making Assistant Try making an informed decision while pushing out a pumpkin! Support people should have a good idea of what may happen during labour in order to help make effective and informed decisions. So read up, tiger!

Celebrity Births

As if celebrity baby names aren't silly enough, the odd celebrity couple has been known to engage in fairly unusual birth practices as well.

Brangelina, not content with adopting a football team from assorted far-flung countries, also decided to have their own daughter, Shiloh, in Namibia. It was a simple affair: heat packs, nice music, massages from Brad, a crack medical team flown in from the US, and the use of the Nigerian government to set up roadblocks and accost and deport unwanted photographers.

In all fairness, the couple did donate the $4.1 million reportedly paid for the exclusive rights to the baby snaps by *People* magazine to an unnamed charity. (Photos, Gran? Sorry, you'll have to buy *People* magazine.)

Tom Cruise and Katie Holmes (free Katie!) opted for a Scientology-style silent birth. The UK's ever-informed *Sun*, among other tabloids, reported that six-foot placards were put up around the birthing suite stating, 'Be silent and make all physical movements slow and understandable.' (Not, 'Stay calm and don't jump on the couch and punch your fists in the air yelling "YEAH!"', as one might expect.)

Scientologists, and presumably Katie Holmes, believe that noise in childbirth may have the effect of scarring the baby's 'reactive mind', a theoretical part of the brain which the church's creator, science-fiction writer L. Ron Hubbard, believed is responsible for most mental and physical illnesses.

Hubbard is also quoted on his birth beliefs in a 1958 newsletter as saying, 'the delivery itself should carry as little anaesthetic as possible, be as calm and no-talk [sic] as possible and the baby should not be bathed or chilled but should be wrapped somewhat tightly in a warm blanket, very soft, and then left alone for a day or so'.

Hmmm.

Dogsbody As mentioned, you should provide your partner with plenty of food and fluids if permitted by your caregiver. Beyond that, basically do anything she asks.

Photojournalist/Cameraman/Documentary Maker Lights, camera, action! It's usually one of your responsibilities to record your child's day of birth. However, if it prevents you from taking an active part in the baby's birth, hand the responsibility over to someone else if possible (but not to some guy you met in the corridor).

Remember to charge the camera, and print or back up the photos as soon as you can. (Theft or loss of a camera will result in your first baby photos disappearing forever, and there won't be a rock big enough to crawl under if this happens!)

Public Relations Specialist Keeping the public notified with email or text releases is an important part of the job, along with progress reports to close members of the family.

The Breaking of the Waters

As mentioned in earlier chapters, your baby is enclosed by a skin-like sac that contains the fabled amniotic fluid. Before the baby can leave the womb, the sac needs to break and the fluid needs to come out, which is known by the rather biblical description of 'the breaking of the waters'.

Contrary to popular belief the breaking of the waters may not be the first thing to happen in labour. They can pop any time! There is quite a lot of fluid and it can come out in a flood, so be prepared!

The First Stage of Labour

Ten to one you will be doing something important when your partner calls to say she is in labour (like playing Yahtzee, fishing or something else that doesn't involve babies). Like Clark Kent, you'll need to change personas, get super-focused and fly home pronto to be by your partner's side.

In the first stage of labour, regular contractions start and slowly build up to a crescendo. The contractions are squeezing open the cervix and pushing the baby into a position where it can be born. This can be a protracted process, particularly in a first labour. It could be hours and hours – which is a long time to make chitchat with people you don't know in a hospital – so ideally a lot of the first stage of labour will be managed by you and other support people at home.

What Triggers Labour?

We can split an atom and send a man to the moon, but we don't really know what triggers labour (which may say something about the direction of scientific funding!).

However, what is generally accepted is that a hormone called prostaglandin prepares the cervix for labour by making it softer and stretchier. Prostaglandin also fires up the womb to make it sensitive to oxytocin, the wonder hormone that makes the uterus contract.

Beyond this there is debate within the medical and scientific communities as to what triggers the process. One school of thought is that it's the presence of surfactant (the lung detergent) excreted from the foetus that lets the mother know the baby is ready, while another belief is that a stress hormone called cortisol is released by the baby after its long internment, thus providing the trigger for birth.

However, until there is consensus among the experts, the trigger for labour will have to remain a mystery.

Managing Before the Cavalry Arrives

In this first stage of labour you're likely to be on your own for a while, so pay heed to the following information to get you through. (And remember, watching the cricket while your partner is in labour can be dangerous to your health.)

While you are at home, the contractions are going to get stronger, more frequent, and sorry to say, more painful. You need to keep your caregiver updated because they will use this information to decide when you need to come to the hospital.

The pain passes, but the beauty remains.

Pierre-Auguste Renoir

OK, scribe, start timing those contractions … You'll need a pen, a piece of paper and a clock with a second hand. Start by recording the length of contractions and the time between contractions in minutes and seconds. Your caregiver will need this information to determine how the labour is progressing.

What Causes Contractions?

The uterus is basically a tube of muscle. During pregnancy it bulks up like a body builder on steroids, increasing in size more than 300 per cent. It also lays down plenty of layers of specialised muscle, and grows metres of new blood vessels to supply the energy to move that baby out of there.

Contractions are kicked off by oxytocin which, released from its holding pen in the brain, floods the womb and gets the party started. Under the influence of oxytocin, muscle cells near the top of the womb start to fire up and behave like the alternator in a car engine by sending waves of electrical currents through the uterus. The muscles in the womb respond to these electrical currents by tightening and gradually getting smaller. These actions then open the cervix, the gateway of the womb, and increase pressure on the womb's contents: the amniotic fluid and bub.

As the pressure increases, the baby seeks the easiest way out, which is through the softened opening of the cervix. The membranes that have contained the baby rupture, the cervix is forced open and, voila! – the baby is squeezed out the birth canal.

To recap and clarify, here's a list of pointers:
- if your partner hasn't phoned the caregiver already, give them a bell and specifically ask them when they want you to come to hospital or when they want you to call them again. (Oh, and follow their instructions!);
- tell your caregiver the frequency and length of your partner's contractions;
- if anything changes, or if you have any concerns, let your caregiver know!;
- if at any stage you're finding it hard to cope, phone another support person to come over and help. There is no shame in the team approach.

Pain Management at Home
If your loved one is starting to find things a bit uncomfortable, offer her pain relief using some of the following common methods.

Pain Management	
Paracetamol	This over-the-counter medication is a great way of starting to manage early labour. Paracetamol inhibits the production of substances that cause pain, swelling and fever. Administer paracetamol only according to the manufacturer's instructions. (Too much paracetamol is very bad for your liver.)
Companionship	Pain has a strong mental or psychic component. If your partner feels that her trusted support person or people are present and are encouraging her, her pain can seem more tolerable.
Warm water	A hot bath or shower can provide excellent pain relief during the first stage of labour. Make sure the water is no hotter than your partner's usual bath or shower.
Hot packs	Hot packs can provide excellent relief during early labour. You can buy commercially made hot packs that are suitable for labour pain. Alternatively, ask your caregiver what they recommend. Just be careful not to make them too hot, as they can burn the skin.
Massage	Massage can be a pain inhibitor, particularly massage to the back, shoulders and neck. You might want to lay off massaging your partner's abdomen – it can over-stimulate the uterus and cause problems.
Freedom of movement	Think about how walking or pacing around helps when you kick your toe.
Help her relax	If your partner can relax, pain may be more easily managed. To encourage this, provide an environment for your partner to relax in through her contractions. Depending on what she finds relaxing, you might like to run her a warm bath or get her some herbal tea.
Distraction	Sometimes doing something your partner enjoys can effectively control pain in the first stage of labour. To help with the pain grab her a book or put on her favourite DVD. While doing something physical can distract from the pain common sense rules, remember please keep your partner off the quad bike and trampoline!

Dealing With Possible Emergencies at Home

Although emergencies at home in the first stage of labour don't happen often, you need to be on the ball. If any of the following events occur, call your caregiver immediately and follow their instructions:

- your partner can't feel the baby moving;
- there is vaginal bleeding (if there are buckets of blood, lie her down and call an ambulance);

- the umbilical cord is hanging out or is in the vagina;
- the waters break and the amniotic fluid is discoloured (anything other than clear or light pink), or it smells really bad;
- your partner is in unbearable pain.

If you think you have a genuine emergency on your hands, call an ambulance and let your caregiver know that you are on your way to hospital.

Treatment With Your Caregiver

So you have called your poor caregiver for the tenth time and they have finally told you to come to hospital. You pack your grimacing partner, her mother and four heavy suitcases into your car and head to the hospital. Hoorah!

Now remember, don't drive at 120 km/h through the streets of your community, screaming at old ladies using the zebra crossing, as this may prevent everyone reaching the hospital in one piece.

Breathe easy, gents, the help has arrived ... or rather, you have arrived to the help. The first

People are giving birth underwater now. They say it's less traumatic for the baby because it's in water. But it's certainly more traumatic for the other people in the pool.

Elayne Boosler

Drug Use During Childbirth May Affect Breastfeeding

A recent study by Siranda Torvaldsen of the University of Sydney suggests that the use of drugs in childbirth may affect a baby's ability to breastfeed.

Assessing a group of 416 women who used the opioid drug fentanyl, administered through epidural injection during childbirth, Torvaldsen's team found that this group was twice as likely to have stopped breastfeeding their babies by six months, as opposed to a control group of 312 women who hadn't used the drug. Torvaldsen couldn't define whether the drugs were affecting the babies' ability to suckle or the mother's ability to supply milk.

thing your caregiver will want to do is make sure your partner and baby are OK and establish how soon you guys are likely to have the little tacker in your arms. This is a good time for you to hand over your birth plan (if you have made one), as this will give them an idea of your expectations of the birth.

The physical check-up performed by your caregiver usually includes:

- listening to the baby's heart rate with a CTG or foetal Doppler;
- checking your partner's blood pressure and recording her temperature;
- working out the position of the baby by feeling your partner's abdomen;
- examining the colour of vaginal loss;
- performing a vaginal examination to find out how far open the cervix is and where the baby is in the birth canal (this is where they talk 'centimetres dilated'). Vaginal examinations will be performed throughout the first stage of labour and are the yardstick to determine how things are progressing.

After this examination your caregiver will generally leave you all to your own devices (unless birth is imminent), popping in and out every once in a while to check on how your partner and baby are doing.

Believe it or not, you're still in the first stage of labour. The support people are of utmost importance at this stage, as they will have to provide the majority of care.

Pain Management With Your Caregiver

While you are running the bath and giving your partner sips of water, your caregiver can be called upon to provide assistance and expert advice. This includes a range of pain-relief options that were not available to you while at home, plus some.

Please note that what is available to your partner also depends on the model of care you have chosen, and how close you guys are to actually having your baby.

Specialised pain-management strategies include the following:

PAIN-RELIEF OPTION	HOW IT WORKS	POSSIBLE SIDE-EFFECTS
Nitrous oxide	Great at the dentist's, abused by teenagers the world over, and frequently used in labour. This short-acting gas can be used to help your partner through contraction pain and is very simple to use: she simply breathes it in via a mouthpiece or mask. Nitrous oxide works by altering the perception of pain. Its advantages are that it is non-toxic to both mother and child, it can be self-regulated by your partner, and the effects wear off very quickly.	• Can cause nausea and vomiting. • Can cause drowsiness or confusion. • If *you* get caught having a go, it can be a very bad look!
Pethidine	This is a man-made drug with a similar chemical structure to morphine. It helps with strong pain and can produce a relaxed state of mind that assists labour. It is given as a needle in the butt, leg or arm.	• Can affect the baby's heart rate and interfere with its desire to breathe, so it should not be used under two hours from birth. • Can cause nausea and vomiting.
Epidural	An epidural is a very effective form of pain relief. An anaesthetist puts a needle into your partner's spine, then withdraws it, leaving a plastic tube in its place. Drugs that make your partner numb from the waist down are then administered through the tube.	• Your partner will be restricted to bed to have the baby. • It can make it harder for the labour to progress, and there is a greater likelihood that your partner may need other treatment to have the baby (see 'Other Ways to Have Your Baby', pages 166–172). • Some of the numbness from the drugs may take a bit of time to wear off, so your partner may need help doing stuff.

Transition

Transition is the name given to the end part of the first stage of labour. It can be a bit intense, as contractions are very strong and very close together, which can provoke an interesting range of emotions and some colourful language from labouring women. Your partner is almost there, but it's not time to push just yet.

This is often the time when your partner may need the most support. She may be at her most confused and irritable, and may be starting to feel that labour is never going to end. At this stage keep in mind the following things:

- support, support, support!;
- if you are concerned about your partner's behaviour, ask your caregiver to assess her;
- don't get upset, no matter what abuse is thrown your way. Remember, it's not you crapping a football.

International Birth Rituals

Common belief in the somewhat wayward state of Bihar, India, is that if a woman's birth is not progressing she should drink a glass of water in which her mother-in-law's big toe has been dipped. (Eeeeeoooh!)

The belief stems from the Ayurvedic assumption that knowledge leaves the body through the feet, the end point being the big toe. Knowledge concerning birth is therefore thought to be transferred from experienced mother-in-law to inexperienced mother-to-be in this way.

Many Hindus practise the ritual of touching elders' feet as a sign of respect, hence the big-toe-in-the-glass-of-water thing is also a sign of respect.

Just make sure she's washed her feet before the big day.

The Central African Republic has a pretty groovy birth ritual which you may want to suggest to your partner, if she has a good singing voice, in times of pain. It's a call-and-response song and it goes like this:

Woman: El-OH mama ti mbi, ti mbi aso mbi.
Birth partner: Kanda be ti MO!
Roughly translated, this means:
Woman: Geez, my belly hurts me.
Birth partner: Well, tough it out, love!

In Guatemala, if a baby is taking its time coming then the solution is to boil a purple onion in beer and have the woman drink the liquid.

In Maharashtra, India, worshippers at a Muslim shrine believe that tossing a newborn in the air in the vicinity of the temple will bring good luck and health to the child. The bubs land and bounce on a taut sheet held by the village men, before being handed back to their mothers. The practice has been going on for 500 years, apparently without injury.

Monitoring the Baby

During the first and second stages of labour it is standard practice that your baby will be monitored in some form to make sure it is doing OK.

There are several ways this can be done, which include:

Foetal Doppler

During uncomplicated vaginal delivery, your baby is monitored with a foetal Doppler, a contraption that listens to the baby's heart rate to see if there is a problem. (See Chapter 4 for more information about the foetal Doppler.)

The CTG (Cardiotocograph)

If your partner is having any kind of medical assistance during the labour she will normally be put on a CTG machine. This machine has two leads, which are strapped to your partner's abdomen. One detects the baby's heart rate and the other detects the strength and frequency of contractions. This can be useful information, especially if you are having an induction of labour with oxytocin. This may restrict your partner's options for birthing, such as water birthing, standing, walking about or adopting different positions.

Foetal Scalp pH Test

If your caregiver thinks your baby might be getting tired, they might suggest a foetal scalp pH test. It's a sure-fire way to determine if the bub is in trouble and is an amazing (if slightly disturbing) procedure.

While your baby is still in the birth canal, a small cut is made on its head and a sample of blood is removed and electrodes are attached to your baby's scalp that monitor its heart rate. This blood is put through a machine that looks at the amount of oxygen and carbon dioxide in the blood. If the baby is stressed, the machine will show the results. Plans can then be made by your caregiver to sort out any problem.

The Second Stage of Labour

Finally, the moment you and your partner have been waiting for! This is it, the big push. Your caregiver will have performed a vaginal examination and told your partner that her cervix has dilated to a magic 10 centimetres.

During the second stage of labour, the contractions and pushing from your partner squeeze your child through the pelvis and down into the birth canal, resulting in the birth of your baby. This sounds simple in theory, but the second stage of labour will take a lot of effort and some time. Generally speaking, your caregiver will stay with your partner throughout the second stage of labour.

Pushing

Women in labour can have really different experiences. For some it's like their body takes over and will do almost instinctively the right thing to help get the baby out. For others labour doesn't go

The Big Head, Little Hip Conundrum

Humans, pah! Although we are an obviously successful species we have more than our share of design flaws, one of the most striking being the size of the heads of our young at birth and the size of the pelvis they must fit through to be born.

The problem occurs because babies' heads tend to be big and women's pelvises tend to be small, making it a tight squeeze for a human child. Even given the best angle at birth, the head only just fits through the pelvis, with a mere centimetre or so to spare.

This rather odd design makes human birth longer and more arduous in comparison to the births of other mammals … although the whole process, biologically speaking, has its advantages. It is theorised that the big squeeze benefits a child by removing excess fluid from its little lungs and helps with the bub's first breath. Evidence to support this is that some caesarean babies, who haven't gone through the big push, can have breathing problems, as amniotic fluid may remain in their lungs.

like that at all. Sometimes a woman will need the direction of a caregiver to tell her when to actively push out the bub. Once the cervix is open it's time for your partner to push out the baby. The pushing motion is similar to that of doing a number two, and although it sounds revolting, this type of pushing is effective. Your caregiver will instruct your partner when to push. These instructions correspond with the contractions.

Positions for Birth and Your Role in Them

Sometimes a caregiver will need your partner to birth the baby in a certain position (like she is has an epidural and can't stand up) but the most part position your partner decides to birth your baby is up to her. Your role as a support person is to be the human gymnasium. Your mission, if you choose to accept it, is to provide a platform for your partner to push out your child. Once again the positions a women will birth in are as individual as they are, but here are some common ones.

Lying in Bed on Her Back or Side

Generally the upper body of the woman needs to be slightly raised to provide a bit of gravity to help the baby out. Women with epidural analgesia often give birth in this position. Support people can be asked to support the woman's legs, hold her hands, supply drinks, mop her brow and provide emotional support between contractions.

Squatting

Squatting on the floor with or without the aid of a birthing stool is an effective method of birthing. It has been shown to reduce prolonged labours but has a slightly increased risk of vaginal tearing. Your main role as a support person during squatting (apart from the emotional support thing) is to support your partner's weight and help her rest in between contractions.

All Fours

An all-fours position to birth can be performed on the floor or in bed, with pillows, a support person or a device like a birthing ball used to support your partner's upper half. In the all-fours position, support people can be human pillows, brow mop, give drinks, and most importantly give her encouragement and remind her she is doing a fabulous job.

Crowning

After a lot of panting, puffing and pushing, your baby should move further along the birth canal and you will see the hair on its head as it travels towards the great outdoors. Often a mirror is used to show your partner that the baby's head is in view, as this provides encouragement for the work ahead. You go, girl!

With a heap more work from your partner, more of the baby's head will slowly inch into sight. When the widest part of the baby's head is visible, the birth of the baby is imminent. This is known as crowning.

NOTE: During crowning it is important that your partner tries not to push the baby out. She needs to listen to the instructions of your caregiver, as pushing during crowning can cause severe vaginal tearing.

The Baby is Born

The baby's head will pop out and the first thing your caregiver will do is make sure the umbilical cord is not wound around its neck. This is sometimes a problem, and if it happens your caregiver will carefully lift the cord over the baby's head to free it for delivery.

After the head is out, the shoulders and body usually follow with the next few contractions. Normally your bub will be placed in your partner's arms or on her chest. This is obviously a very emotional time for everyone, and generally a few tears are shed.

At this stage your caregiver might invite you to cut the umbilical cord (don't cut your caregiver's fingers!). An injection of artificial

I will be joining the campaign with a song in my heart, with a spring in my step.

Charles Kennedy, on the birth of his first child

Prayer to the Egyptian frog goddess:

O Heqat, hasten this birth.

Westcar Papyrus

oxytocin (syntocinon) is usually given to your partner immediately after the birth. This helps prevent postpartum haemorrhage.

Care of the Baby Immediately After Birth

Once the baby is out, the little one is usually given a vigorous rub by your caregiver to stimulate its breathing into action.

Next, your baby is checked at the first minute and the fifth minute to see how it is breathing, to check its colour and to listen to how its heart is beating. This is all added up and your child is given what is known as an Apgar (named after the anaesthetist who invented it) score out of ten.

Sometimes the baby will need some assistance, and other caregivers may become involved. Specialised equipment can be used to help the baby breathe, stay warm and adapt to the outside world.

Vaginal Tearing and Repair

Sorry to have to talk about this, but you may have some interest in the future condition of your partner's vagina, so it is therefore important that you know a little bit about vaginal repair.

While some women can be lucky and come through this unscathed, the vagina can often come out a little worse for wear after the whole birth thing.

The damage sustained can range from simple grazing and bruising through to severe tearing of the perineum (the skin

How Does a Newborn Stay Warm?

Up until the time of birth, your little one has been living the life of Riley, relying on Mum for food, oxygen and for keeping warm. The normal temperature in the womb is about 37.7 degrees Celsius, like a nice warm bath. But following birth, wherever it arrives, the child is exposed to atmospheric temperature. To cope with this, special receptors in the brain that measure temperature send messages to heat-regulating centres in the brain to fire up the thermostats. The healthy baby is henceforth able to maintain an even body temperature.

How Do Babies Breathe Once They're Out?

In the womb your little one has practised breathing for months. Muscles have been strengthened and nerve pathways have been laid down. As labour begins and your bub is squeezed from the womb, the amniotic fluid that has been sitting in the lungs is also squeezed out, which is a pretty bloody good design.

So now the lungs are empty and ready … but they need a chemical trigger to fire them into action. That trigger is the fact that once the umbilical cord ceases to supply oxygen via placental blood, carbon dioxide, a by-product of energy production, starts to build up. This in turn creates a biochemical crisis as the carbon dioxide combines with water to form acid. As it happens, it's a necessary crisis, as the acid build-up sends messages to the brain, muscles are kicked into action, and lo and behold, your baby takes its first breath.

and muscle between the vagina and anus). Most vaginal damage will require stitches. The best repairs are done with absorbable suturing material put in by an experienced vaginal mechanic. In extreme cases, vaginal repair will require surgery.

NOTE: During certain emergency procedures the vagina is cut (called an episiotomy) to help release a baby or to give caregivers more working room. This should not be confused with routine episiotomy which was performed in the 'good old days' to prevent tearing.

It is thought by most caregivers today that if a tear is to happen, the best healing comes from tearing along natural lines of stress. So the new approach is generally *not* to cut.

The Third Stage of Labour

Oh no, it's not over yet! The third and final stage of this whole to-do involves the delivery of the placenta. After the baby is born, light contractions continue. These cause the placenta to move down to the bottom of the uterus and pass out of the vagina.

Attack of the Giant Babies

Don't let your partner read this, but there are actually giant babies being born around the world as we speak. The average birth weight of girls in Australia is about 3.25 kilograms and the average length is 49 centimetres, while boys come in at about 3.5 kilograms and 50 centimetres in length. However, there are some much bigger ones out there.

In Townsville, Queensland, in July 2009, Chelsea Rose Mackay, weighing 6.28 kilograms and measuring 55 centimetres in length, came in as one of the largest babies born in the country. Chelsea had to be fitted into clothes for three- to six-month olds.

Other recent giant bubs include one born in Sumatra, Indonesia, in September 2009, who entered the world with a resounding thud at 8.6 kilograms. According to the *Guiness Book of Records*, the biggest baby ever born was birthed by Carmelina Fedele from Italy and tipped the scales at 10.3 kilograms. Egad!

The causes of big babies can be related to genetics or to the fact that the mother suffered gestational diabetes, which caused too much sugar to cross the placenta and thus overfed the baby. If a baby is predicted to be very large, your caregiver may recommend a caesarean.

61 cm
8.6 kg

Giant
Sumatran Baby

Average
Australian
Baby
Girls and Boys
Averaged

49.5 cm
3.4 kg

Often your caregiver will apply a little gentle traction on the umbilical cord to assist with the delivery of the placenta. Expect quite a lot of blood.

The placenta is then examined to make sure it looks normal and is complete.

Possible Serious Stuff to Worry About in Labour

Hey … hold on. My partner's in labour! I'm too stressed already to have anything go wrong. Sadly gents sometimes it does and the medical problems in labour and birth can be whoppers.

Foetal Distress

Ironically, the day of a baby's birth can be one of the most arduous in its life. For a range of reasons, some babies become deprived of oxygen and their heart rate goes up. After a period of time they can become tired, and this can spell trouble.

In this situation they may need help, and quickly. This usually means that delivery has to be speeded up, therefore your child may well be born by caesarean or with the aid of instruments (forceps or suction cup – see pages 167–168).

In some situations the baby may be very unwell at birth and will need to be transferred to a neonatal intensive care unit for specialised treatment.

Postpartum Haemorrhage

Women bleed when they have babies, and normally this isn't too much of a problem. Postpartum haemorrhage is defined as excessive bleeding (greater than 500 millilitres) in the 24 hours following birth. If undetected, this kind of heavy bleeding may lead to serious problems.

Undetected bleeding is a major cause of serious illness for women having babies in Australia, as sometimes the womb hasn't contracted properly following birth or there are ruptured blood vessels. Whatever the cause, early identification of the problem is vital, as is correcting this dangerous complication.

You have a role to play to ensure your partner's safety. If she complains of heavy bleeding or wetness between her legs, if she feels light-headed or close to fainting, get her examined promptly.

Medication may be needed to contract her uterus, or a blood transfusion and surgery may be necessary in severe cases.

Prolonged Labour

This is defined as a labour that lasts too long, leading to an extremely tired, dehydrated partner and a distressed baby. Your caregiver will decide to speed up the birth through augmentation with oxytocin, the use of instruments or you may need a caesarean.

Shoulder Dystocia

Very rarely a baby's shoulder gets stuck under the pelvis as it's making its way out. This situation is not good, as the baby can't go forward and can't go backwards. If the little mite remains stuck it will be deprived of oxygen and could die. There are things your caregiver can do to release the baby and you may be asked to help. If this should happen, follow their instructions promptly!

You may be asked to support if your partners legs and push in upwards towards her chest, or help you caregiver get your partner into an all-fours position which can help release a trapped baby.

Retained Placenta

Generally in the third stage of labour the expulsion of the placenta happens without any dramas. However, there are instances where part of the membranes or the placenta is left behind following birth, which is why your caregiver checks it thoroughly following its eviction. If there is any retained placenta, your partner is at greater risk of developing postpartum haemorrhage or an infection.

If this should happen your partner may be allowed some time to pass the placenta piece naturally or may have to have an operation to remove it.

Cord Prolapse

As you may have experienced, electrical cords and garden hoses have an annoying habit of getting everywhere. The same thing sometimes happens with the umbilical cord. Once the waters have broken, the cord sometimes heads down the birth canal ahead of the baby, which can cause serious oxygen-supply problems to the baby.

Mile Cry Club

Although relatively rare, there are recorded circumstances where babies have been born mid-flight. One was on a British Airways flight in September 2006. Young Nadine was born six weeks prematurely to an Egyptian mother travelling on a US passport, flying between the UK and Canada on a British-owned plane. Young Nadine and the mother were fine, but how were they to determine the place of birth?

The United Nations specifies that children who are born on planes should take the origin of birth of the country that the plane is registered to. However, place of birth and citizenship are two different things, and in this area countries have different laws and regulations.

The US, for example, grants citizenship if a child is born over US air space, while in Australia it's a bit more perplexing. In NSW, if a child is born on a flight to Sydney from anywhere in the country, the birth is registered in NSW. The same thing applies in Queensland, as long as the child hasn't stopped anywhere before reaching Queensland. Confusingly, the Australian *Citizenship Act* of 1948, states that 'A person born on a registered ship or aircraft shall be deemed to have been born at the place at which the ship or aircraft was registered'. They do make it clear, however, that citizenship to Australia is only granted if one of the parents is an Australian citizen.

On another contentious matter, if a baby is born on a plane, is there any truth to the persistent rumour that the child is entitled to free flights on the carrier for the rest of his or her life? Internet myth-buster www. snopes.com reports that the carrier has no commitment to provide this service (though on at least two occasions, media-savvy airlines *have* granted special flight privileges and educational scholarships to babies born mid-flight).

So if you're thinking of timing your labour for that overseas trip, folks, think twice. The chances of getting something out of it are pretty slim, and surely not worth the discomforts or risks of giving birth mid-air. Besides, for most international flights you will be limited as to when in your pregnancy you can travel.

Different airlines have different rules for carrying pregnant women. Aussie carrier Qantas specifies that for domestic travel there is no restriction for a normal uncomplicated pregnancy, but medical clearance is required if you wish to travel past the 36th week for an uncomplicated multiple pregnancy. International travel is not permitted after the 36th week for routine pregnancies or the 32nd week for routine multiple pregnancies.

Your caregiver will push up the baby's head giving the cord some room for the blood supply to get to the baby. Then your partner will need an emergency caesarean.

Postpartum Infection

Sometimes after a baby is born an infection develops. It often originates in the uterus and is a result of some retained placenta or amniotic sac. Infection like this can affect the whole body and needs to be promptly identified and treated with antibiotics. Some women who develop serious postpartum infections may require some time in an intensive care unit to recover.

Meconium Aspiration

Sometimes a baby gets so stressed in labour that it poos on the way out. This can be a problem, as the baby's lungs can get full of faeces, causing respiratory distress and later infections. If this happens to your baby, it may need help breathing and some further treatment in an intensive care unit.

Other Ways to Have Your Baby

Although having babies has been going on for a while, sometimes old Mother Nature doesn't get it right and a woman needs assistance from the medical world. On occasions when babies become distressed, or when labour is taking too long, or when there are other medical complications, alternative approaches to birth are needed. These interventions may not be what you guys planned, but they might be necessary to try and make things safe for your partner and baby.

Some women might feel like they have failed by not having a normal vaginal delivery, or by deviating from the birth plan. Remember to be sympathetic to your partner and try to reassure her that she hasn't failed.

Following are techniques which may be used to assist with birth.

Augmented Labour

Sometimes your caregiver may decide the contractions need a little more 'oomph' to help the labour along, in which case a drip with artificial oxytocin (called syntocinon) may be started to increase the effectiveness of contractions.

This can be rather painful for the woman, as the contractions can come fast and furiously. CTG monitoring will be used to monitor your baby and the contractions. Augmented labour usually restricts your partner's birthing to a bed and limits her options for pushing the bub out.

The use of oxytocin infusions carries a range of risks, as mentioned in 'Drugs To Bring On Labour' in Chapter 5, but is generally considered very safe.

Forceps Delivery

Forceps look like giant salad tongs and are designed to cradle the head of the baby, allowing your caregiver to help the baby descend into the birth canal. Sometimes your caregiver may suggest you opt for a forceps delivery. They are fantastic instruments to get out a distressed baby and in the hands of a skilled operator are life-savers.

Complications for Mum can include:
• injury to cervix, vagina or perineum;
• postpartum haemorrhage (from above trauma);
• pain during passing urine;
Complications for Baby can include:
• marks and bruising on the face;
• an increased risk of jaundice due to facial bruising;
• facial nerve damage (usually temporary).

Vacuum Extraction (Ventouse)

Another type of instrumental delivery is with the suction cup, or ventouse. This rather interesting device looks like it should belong to a plumber. It serves the same function as forceps but is based on a sink-plunger design rather than on salad tongs. The cup is placed on the head of the baby, a little suction is applied and the baby is assisted down the birth canal.

Complications for Mum can include:
• vaginal trauma;
• PPH (from above truma).
Complications for Baby can include:
• scalp trauma and bruising;
• increased risk of jaundice from bruising.

Caesarean (C-section)

This is the well-known surgical procedure wherein the abdomen and uterus are opened to facilitate the removal of your baby.

There are a range of good medical reasons for this surgical procedure, which may include any of the following.

Reasons for Mum:
- severe pre-eclampsia or eclampsia;
- big baby (increased risk of shoulder dystocia);
- active herpes in the mother.

Reasons for Baby:
- severe Rhesus disease;
- breech position;
- small baby, or a baby that has had problems growing;
- foetal distress.

Reasons for both Mum and Baby:
- failure to progress in labour;
- antepartum haemorrhage;
- placenta praevia.

What Goes on in a Caesarean and the Man's Part in It!

Firstly you will be asked to change into a stylish pair of theatre pyjamas. Your partner will have an epidural inserted and will be taken into the operating room and prepared for the operation. When this has been done, you will be ushered in to sit with her. Your partner will be awake during the operation, unless it's an emergency.

The obstetrician will start to cut through the seven layers of skin, muscle and womb to reach your baby. Mercifully, you won't be able to see the operation, as your view will be obscured by drapes. Your baby is born from the cut in your partner's abdomen and handed to the paediatrician and/or midwife to check that it is doing OK. After this, you will be invited to see and hold the baby, and to show it to your partner.

You and the baby will generally be sent to the postnatal ward to wait for your partner while she is sewn up and sent to a recovery room. After she is stable, she will be wheeled to the postnatal ward to join you and your new addition to the family.

Cautionary note: The operating theatre is a bizarre world unto itself, with its own rules. As a visitor you will be expected to follow instructions promptly and to not touch anything without asking first!

If the wheels really start falling off during the whole labour thing, your partner may be sent for a dyed-in-the-wool emergency

Caesareans: Myths and Milestones

If your baby is born via caesarean it is in good company, as there are a host of mythological and historical figures who have made their way into existence via the ol' C-section. Julius Caesar, the bald adulterer, is thought by some to be the inspiration for the name caesarean, as some historians have suggested the great Roman leader was born via C-section.

In Greek mythology, when the god Apollo discovered his pregnant girlfriend, the nymph Coronis, had been unfaithful to him, he went mad and organised his sister to bump her off with an arrow. As Coronis lay on her funeral pyre, Apollo performed a quick caesarean and pulled out his child, Asklepios, who later (quite appropriately) became the Greek god of medicine.

Not to be outdone, it is also thought that Dionysus, Greek god of wine and revelry, was also delivered by C-section. Meanwhile, over on the Indian subcontinent, Buddha was said to have been born 'from his mother's side', and Brahman, a Hindu deity, was born from his mother's umbilical cord(!).

King Robert II of Scotland (1316–1390) was also born by caesarean and may have been the inspiration for the hero Macduff in Shakespeare's *Macbeth* ('from his mother's womb untimely ripp'd').

While good has entered the world via C-section, so, if you want to believe it, has evil. A series of woodcuts from the fifteenth century show the anti-Christ being born from the incised abdomen of his mother.

Perhaps the first successful caesarean (by modern standards) was performed in Switzerland around 1500 when a pig surgeon, Jacob Nufer, realised his wife was in trouble. She had been in labour for days and had been seen by thirteen midwives, to no avail. The desperate Jacob used his pig-surgery skills to perform a caesarean on his wife. (This was before anaesthetics, so it would have been quiet a big deal for her!) Amazingly, the surgery was a complete success. The baby lived to be 77, and Jacob's wife went on to have five other children, including a set of twins. Good one, Jacob!

C-section. She will be put under a general anaesthetic and you will not be invited into the operating theatre. (You will be shown a quiet place to wait instead.)

Safety and Complications of Caesareans

For women and babies with legitimate medical issues, C-sections are life-saving. However, a C-section is not without its complications. In the first place, it is major abdominal surgery, and any major surgery carries risks – like bleeding, infection and constipation to name a few. In the second place, a caesarean prevents the normal adaptive processes that occur when a child is born via the vagina.

Risks for the mother may include:
- postpartum haemorrhage;
- postoperative infection;
- pulmonary embolism (a blood clot in the lungs).

Risks for the baby may include:
- breathing problems;
- difficulty getting feeding established.

Your Partner After the Operation

After a caesarean your partner will, as already mentioned, be sent to a recovery room where she will be observed for signs of complications. If all goes well, she will be wheeled to the postnatal ward to be reunited with you and the baby. Different hospitals have different routines, but generally, following a caesarean, you should expect the following:

- for the first days your partner will be in bed, bombed-out on painkillers. She will be sleepy and generally feel like crap;
- she will have a urinary catheter (a tube going into her bladder) inserted so she doesn't have to get up to go to the loo. This will be taken out after a day or so;
- on day two your partner will be helped from bed, and over the next few days she will become more mobile and will be able to do more things for the baby;
- once you all leave hospital, there are restrictions on your partner on driving a car, lifting and walking up stairs. If you can't be at home to help, make sure she has friends or family present to give her the assistance she needs;

Alternative Births Explained

If your partner's a bit on the hippie side, then here's a rundown on the latest new-age-y-type births that you might be talked into. If you're a bit of a hippie yourself, then it might give you some ideas.

Water Birthing

Not strictly a new-age practice, as many women may experience parts of their labour in a bath or birth pool, however some women choose to actually give birth to their babies under water.

The practice is not as dangerous as it sounds, as the baby gets all the oxygen it needs through the umbilical cord and does not need to breathe through its mouth until it comes into contact with air, which provides a trigger for the breathing reflex.

The benefits for mothers may include increased relaxation throughout the birth process, more comfortable support for the body, and possibly a reduction in the pain of labour.

For so-called water babies, water births are supposed to be more gentle than regular births. The bubs themselves are reported as being calmer, more relaxed and happier than normal terrestrial babies.

Lotus Birthing

In a lotus birth the baby's umbilical cord is left attached to the placenta until it dries up and falls off two to ten days later. A tad labour-intensive, the placenta is placed in a 'placenta bag' and needs to be salted periodically to keep it dry.

The practice was first conceived by Clair Lotus Day in 1974 after she observed the behaviour in chimpanzees and reasoned that their practices might be advantageously adopted by humans. (Strangely, she had no desire to give birth in a tree.)

Although evidence is fairly anecdotal, lotus birth proponents firmly believe that their babies are noticeably happier, calmer and more relaxed, that they lose less weight after birth, and that they have less chance of experiencing breastfeeding jaundice in the first week after birth.

Freebirthing

WHOOO, yeah! Let's do this thing!

Sounding a bit like an extreme sport, freebirthing is the practice of giving birth out of the hospital surrounds without any medical help.

Freebirthing is part of the backlash against the over-medicalisation of birth. Its proponents and practitioners believe that the presence of medical workers interrupts the natural flow of childbirth. Obvious disadvantages, as loudly expressed by the medical fraternity, are that the practice can be dangerous to both mother and child, particularly in circumstances where there are complications.

• it takes about four to six weeks to fully recover from a
caesarean.

A New Baby ... What Now?

Your baby is out. They are finally out. This is the point you
should get on your knees to thank your partner (also to thank
god you're not a woman and will never need to go through that!)
then give that baby a cuddle!

Baby Check and Vital Statistics

After everyone has had a cuddle of the baby, he or she needs to
be checked over by your caregiver to see if there are any physical
problems that require medical attention. Babies are also weighed,
labelled, measured, dressed and wrapped.

Having a Baby in a Neonatal Intensive Care Unit

If your baby is born early or there have been complications
during birth, it may be sent to a neonatal intensive care unit –
which is a great place for very sick babies but can be stressful
for parents.

These units are full of strange machines buzzing, beeping
and flashing, busy, clever people running around being
important, and somewhere in the middle, your baby in a big
plastic box. Your partner may be unwell or needing a lot of
support at this time, so you might be in charge of visiting
your baby.

Even though you might be a little shell-shocked, try to
establish a rapport with the doctors and nurses looking after
your baby. They are the best source of information about
what is happening with your baby.

Some of the things you might want to ask are:
• What is wrong with my baby?
• How long will my baby be in intensive care?
• What will be involved in my baby's treatment and daily
  care?
• What medicines will my baby have to take?
• What types of tests will be done?
• What can I do to help my baby?
• Will my baby have any lasting problems?

Feeding
Once the baby is out it will be hungry and will need a feed. Colostrum is the first milk produced by your partner. It is high in protein and is rich with antibodies, and just the ticket for a little bub when first born! If your partner isn't going to breastfeed, it's time for the baby's first bottle (see 'Feeding Babies', pages 197–203).

Vitamin K
Vitamin K is important in ensuring the clotting of our blood, but for some reason humans aren't born with enough and we don't get it from breast milk, so newborns are given a dose at birth.

There are two ways to receive vitamin K, either via drops in the mouth or an injection in the thigh. If you decide to administer vitamin K via the mouth, your baby will need to receive three doses rather than just one. Babies that don't receive vitamin K are at risk of bleeding.

Movin' On ...
OK so you've studied up and you're prepared, don't worry you'll get through it and everything will be allright. Of course, you know that one of the most essential and important things you'll have to do is ... Hang on, is that moaning in the background?

Cord Blood and Stem Cells:
The Low-down

Cord blood contains a potent form of stem cell which can perpetually produce white and red blood cells and platelets found in circulating blood. Approximately 90 millilitres of blood can be collected from the umbilical cord vein after delivery without harm or disturbance to the mother or baby. The blood can then be frozen indefinitely without losing its efficacy, and can be later used in bone marrow transplants to treat degenerative diseases such as leukaemia, cancer, immune deficiencies, aplastic anaemias and thalassaemias (provided an appropriate match is found).

With your partner's permission, the blood from the umbilical cord can be donated for public use for someone needing a bone marrow transplant.

Cord blood can also be stored by a private company (at cost) for future use, in the event that the child in later life contracts a disease requiring a bone marrow transplant, or that the stem cells contained in the blood may be used in as-yet undiscovered cures for other diseases.

What Are Stem Cells?

There are two main types of stem cells: embryonic stem cells, which are sometimes called unlimited stem cells (these are found in the placenta, umbilical cord blood and in embryos), and adult stem cells, which are sometimes called limited stem cells (these are found in certain areas of adult tissues or organs).

Embryonic stem cells have the incredible ability to self-renew and divide into other stem cells – and, most significantly, differentiate themselves into any mature cell or tissue type. An embryonic stem cell could be likened to a seed, which, given the right stimulus and environment, could grow into any type of plant: palm tree, rose bush or eucalyptus. Although stem cells have only been used in bone marrow transplants to date, they offer future potential to reverse numerous diseases and injuries, and give scientists help in developing drugs to prevent diseases.

Adult stem cells are similar undifferentiated cells found in the body. They aid in the regeneration of cells and organ tissue. These cells have similar qualities to embryonic stem cells but are less potent in their ability to differentiate into differing cell types.

There is worldwide controversy surrounding embryonic stem cell research, particularly where the cells are derived from donated embryos from IVF treatments. This is because the process involves the destruction of these embryos and the use of therapeutic cloning, a technique used to make the cells replicate themselves.

Major arguments from opponents cite that the embryos are in fact growing human beings and therefore the process is tantamount to abortion, and that the practice may lead to reproductive cloning and the manipulation of human beings. Researchers argue that the benefits of such research far outweigh these arguments and that the embryos used would be destroyed anyway.

If a Baby Dies

Even with all the money and expertise that is poured into childbirth in Australia, it's a sad fact that some babies are stillborn or die soon after birth. Most commonly these babies have serious issues that have been identified before the birth, but some babies simply don't make it through labour and birth.

This is a time of immense grief for the mother and father, as well as for the extended family of the baby. Staff in hospitals can put families in touch with social workers who can organise counselling and practical assistance. Staff should also be able to provide the grieving family with a 'Memories Box' containing the handprint, a locket of hair and other personal items from the baby.

There are also groups like SIDS Australia that can put a grieving family in touch with others who have lost a baby, to assist them through the experience.

Useful Contacts

The Bub Hub (AUS)

www.bubhub.com.au
Generalised pregnancy and birth contacts and information including a list of outlets that hire birthing equipment.

King Edward Memorial Hospital (WA)

www.kemh.health.wa.gov.au
Web-based information on labour, birth and newborn care.

The Bonnie Babes Foundation (AUS)

www.bbf.org.au
Tel: 1300 266 643 (grief counselling)
A non-profit organisation that provides support and advice for families experiencing loss from miscarriage, stillbirth and premature birth.

7

The Real Deal
After the Birth Checklist

☑ Download or develop birth photos/video.

☑ If you've decided to keep the placenta, put it in the freezer (clearly labelled!) until you're ready to do something with it.

☑ Consider the benefits of breastfeeding and encourage your partner to choose this feeding option, if possible.

☑ Once your partner and baby arrive home, provide as much domestic support as possible.

☑ As always, keep an eye out for any signs of serious medical complications for your partner and baby in the weeks after delivery, but don't get overly anxious about the possibility of problems.

☑ Get ready for a life of sleepless nights, school interviews and pregnancy scares.

☑ Get ready to sit staring with mouth open at the little one for hours on end.

So. Phew! Aren't you glad that's over?

Yes, it was a bit embarrassing that you mistook the afterbirth for some sort of monster twin, and no, there wasn't an instruction manual anywhere to be found, although you spent a lot of time looking.

B-day has come and gone, and now you and your partner find yourself staring in wonder at the little bundle of joy you have created and wondering what on earth you're supposed to do now. This is particularly relevant to you as a man, as in actual fact you're probably going to be feeling a bit like a third wheel for a while.

You have now entered the Baby Zone, a sleepless nether world where everything stops for about three months and revolves around your burping, pooing, crying and mostly ever-so-cute offspring. It's actually best to regard the pregnancy as being 12 months long, as for the three months after their great entry, babies are pretty much inseparable from your partner – sorry, their mother.

You will now realise why you have never seen newborn babies lying on bench presses, nestled between surfboards or dozing in the public bars of reputable hotels. You will also realise why the majority of your friends with young babies are quite hard to cajole into leaving the house. Quite simply, babies and the-things-you-used-to-do-and-took-for-granted don't really match up.

This is something that most men find hard to adapt to. But fear not, you'll get over it soon, and the rewards far outweigh the disadvantages.

Watch Your Foot in Mouth

Never has there been more ample opportunity for you to put your foot in your mouth (and thus encourage your partner to put her foot somewhere else) than in the newborn 'scene'.

Worse than asking a non-pregnant women how many months pregnant she is (embarrassing, but you'll probably never see the woman again), making sweeping opinionated statements concerning children's upbringing can bring about longer-lasting social stigma, as chances are you'll probably be seeing these people

Baby Sign Language

Something that you might run into is the relatively recent trend of baby sign language (BSL), which is basically what it sounds like: a sign language you can teach your baby.

The idea behind BSL is that young babies lack the ability to communicate verbally but that their hand–eye coordination develops a lot faster, thus allowing them to learn basic sign language to communicate. The language includes simple words such as 'eat', 'sleep', 'more', 'hug', 'play', 'cookie' and 'teddy bear'. As yet, signs for 'antidisestablishmentarianism', 'savings account' and 'Daddy is stressed' have not been developed.

Proponents of the use of BSL claim that it allows babies and toddlers to express what they are thinking, thus creating happier bubs and parents, and increases the speed of early literary skills. Babies can apparently start to learn to sign between six and eight months, and teaching usually starts with three to five sign words. The idea is to show the sign and repeat the word while making eye contact with the infant.

again at mothers' groups (yes, guys go to these too), playgrounds, day-care centres or kids' parties for years to come.

Here are some things you may feel tempted to say:

- 'Baby sign language is a waste of time. I mean, isn't pointing to the mouth a good enough indication that the kid is hungry?';
- 'Paying $150 to take your baby to swimming lessons, just to sing songs in the water with a bunch of other suckers, is a waste of money. Give me the kid; I'll take it for a swim for free!';
- 'Spending $60 on a T-shirt smaller than a tea towel with "Give Peas a Chance" or "Muthasucker" written on the front is something only an imbecile or grandparent would do.'

Baby sign language for 'mother-in-law'.

www.commons.wikimedia.org

No matter how obviously stupid you find the litany of baby

Wetting the Baby's Head

Since at least the 1600s, the Old English term 'to wet' (or *weten*) has been used to describe the celebration of an event by drinking alcohol. 'Wetting the baby's head' is a time-honoured tradition that may have its origins in the Christian baptism rites, where the priest physically wetted the head during baptism.

In traditional Australian culture this rite has been adapted somewhat, and the father (while the mother is still in hospital) goes to the pub and tells his mates that his child has been born. His friends respond with congratulations and drink to the health of the baby, thus giving an informal baptism (albeit in the absence of the child and mother).

The origin of the role of cigars in wetting the baby's head remains somewhat uncertain.

It is thought that a North American Indian ceremony, known as the 'potlatch', was the inspiration for the cigars. Others disagree, believing that the use of tobacco to celebrate childbirth had its origins in Spanish Cuba. Regardless of its history, smoking cigars after the birth of one's child became popular in the United States of America and has spread the world over.

To organise your wetting-of-the-baby's-head celebration, you need:
- some mates;
- a nice pub, preferably your local;
- a toast to welcome the baby into the world;
- some cigars.

NOTE: A big night is optional.
NOTE ALSO: This may be your last night out for some time!

stuff expounded by those around you, don't express these inner thoughts in public. Yes, the above is all true, but keep in mind that the moment you express these thoughts publicly, two-thirds of the people you are talking to will be teaching the aforementioned sign language to their infant while doing swimming classes with babies wearing ridiculously expensive T-shirts, accompanied by the babies' grandparents. Try talking your way out of that one! You have been warned.

Your Partner, Post-baby

Your partner's body has been a human incubator, stretched and poked and kicked for 40 weeks. She has put up with nausea, back pain and God-knows-what-else as the baby grew. Then, to top it all off, her body has been pushed almost beyond the bounds of human endurance during labour and birth. She's done amazing things.

But admit it, there is no way her body could have put up with a battering like this and come out the same, is there? Well, you'd be amazed at the postnatal body's recuperative powers.

There is a technical term for the six-week period after your child's birth: it's called the puerperium (try saying it three times quickly after a few beers!). This is the period in which the organs of reproduction are returning to normal.

It starts with the birth of the placenta and is meant to end with your partner's first menstrual period after the birth. Some women (like those breastfeeding or from non-Caucasian backgrounds) can go a long time (more than the 6 weeks) but medical science considers the puerperium finished after six weeks regardless.

If your partner has had a C-section, barring complications like infection, she should be almost fully recovered at the end of the puerperium.

If your partner has had vaginal tearing or an episiotomy it may take a number of weeks to fully heal. As a rule the greater the tear, the longer the healing time.

Uterus

What a mighty organ! It's done its job and now it's time to shut up shop and return to its original size. This shrinking of the uterus occurs as a result of oxytocin (again!), which is released in labour and during breastfeeding.

The extra muscles and blood vessels built up in the uterus during pregnancy are broken down, and over the course of several days the

It is not a slight thing when those so fresh from God love us.
Charles Dickens

A baby will make love stronger, days shorter, nights longer, bankroll smaller, home happier, clothes shabbier, the past forgotten, and the future worth living for.
Anonymous

Oxytocin, Breastfeeding and Bleeding After Birth

Mother Nature has got it going on, and this is never more evident than with oxytocin. As we have seen, the 'love drug' has a relationship with contractions in labour, but being an all-rounder the wonder hormone also has a role in breastfeeding and the prevention of bleeding after the baby is born.

In breastfeeding mothers, oxytocin causes milk to be released from where it is made in the mammary glands so it can be supplied to the hungry baby. This is known as the letdown reflex.

At the same time, the oxytocin released by nipple stimulation during breastfeeding is having an effect on the uterus, causing it to contract, thereby reducing the risk of postpartum haemorrhage.

Clever, huh?

womb will become a hard ball in the lower part of your partner's abdomen. After a few weeks the womb, like a jack-in-the-box put back in its box, will disappear into the pelvic cavity, only to spring forth again at the time of your partner's next pregnancy.

Vaginal Bleeding

Your partner can expect to have bleeding and vaginal discharge for between three and six weeks after the birth. As a rough guide she can expect:

- about one to three days of bleeding (this can be heavier than a period; if it is much heavier, or if she passes big blood clots, get it checked out);
- approximately four to ten days of pinkish discharge;
- some weeks of pinky-brown and whitish discharge.

If this discharge becomes offensive-smelling or your partner gets a fever, she must get it investigated. A large bleed can occur weeks after the birth; if she does have one, consult with your caregiver, or if it's extremely heavy take your partner to hospital, by ambulance if necessary (see 'Postpartum Haemorrhage', pages 163–164).

Breasts

Following the birth of your baby your partner's breasts are going to swell like bowling balls. While it's good to look at it can be painful for your partner. The swelling is mainly caused by increased blood supply and can be relieved by applying cold compresses (get a disposable nappy, add water then freeze) to your partner's long-suffering breasts. This should relieve the swelling.

However, she is not out of the woods in the breast department. Once normal milk production commences around day three your partner's breasts can become engorged with milk. To relieve this your partner can express her breasts or feed the baby.

It is not uncommon for your partner's breasts to feel a bit battered and sore once the baby has started breastfeeding. (*You* try having a small but very determined limpet suck at your nipples between eight and fifteen times a day!)

If her nipples become grazed, cracked or damaged, it's important she sees her caregiver if still in hospital, or GP or early-childhood nurse if she has returned home. This is important, as damaged nipples may lead to mastitis (see page 187).

Care for Your Partner After Birth

In the three to four days following delivery, your partner will be checked at least daily by a midwife to ensure she is going OK. Then at the end of her stay in hospital she will be seen by your chosen caregiver to ensure everything is satisfactory.

About six weeks after returning home, your partner will need to see her GP or go to a Women's Health Centre, Family Planning Centre or maternity caregiver to make sure everything is continuing well. At this appointment, contraception may be discussed, there should be some assessment of her return to a non-pregnant state, a pap (cervical) smear may be offered if due, and a breast check undertaken.

The midwife will:
- make sure your partner's uterus is shrinking as it should;
- check the amount of vaginal bleeding;
- look for signs of infection;
- check your partner's breasts for nipple damage;
- assess vaginal healing.

Tests for Your Baby

Before you go home from the hospital, your baby will need to undertake a few tests, as detailed below.

Hearing Test

It is thought that about 1–2 in 1000 babies are born with a serious hearing problem. This hospital test is really important, as the sooner a hearing problem is identified the sooner it can be dealt with.

Genetic Screening Test

This test needs to be done within 48–72 hours after birth. A midwife will prick your child's heel, obtaining a small amount of blood to test for 30 or so rare genetic diseases that may affect your baby. Parents are only contacted with their child's results if there are any issues.

Hepatitis B Vaccine

Hepatitis B is a nasty disease that Australia is doing its best to eradicate. Your baby will be asked to do its part before you leave hospital by receiving its first hep B vaccine. This is optional and you have the right to refuse. An injection is given into your child's leg … and yes, it hurts, but it's for the good of your child and the country!

Paediatrician's Check

A paediatrician will usually check your baby over to make sure it has no glaring problems prior to leaving. The check includes your baby's heart, its hips and pretty much everything else!

Discharge Weight

Your bub's weight will be taken before you leave the building. It is normal for a baby to lose a bit of weight before discharge, but if your little

My best birth control now is just to leave the lights on.

Joan Rivers

One generation plants the trees; another gets the shade.

Chinese proverb

one has lost more than is average, this is a problem and you may need to stay longer. The extended stay is to establish feeding and to explore other reasons for weight loss.

Early-childhood Nurse Appointment

Before you leave hospital you will usually be given the contact details to make an appointment with an early-childhood nurse at your community health centre. This appointment occurs at within a week to 10 days after returning home. The nurse will check over the baby to make sure all's still going well. He or she will also provide your little tacker with immunisations and other basic healthcare.

As your child grows, community health centres provide a range of good, free services that you may need: kids' dentists, dieticians and free mental health counselling for the new parents, amongst other things.

Possible Serious Stuff for Your Partner After the Baby is Born

Postnatal Depression

It's normal for a woman to feel a bit flat for a few weeks after the baby is born. After all she has lost blood, done the physical equivalent of climbing Mount Everest during labour and has been woken at least 20 times a night to feed the baby since then. This is called the baby blues and will normally settle down. Postnatal depression is something else.

This is a very serious problem and it is said to affect between 15 and 20 per cent of new mothers. There is a lot of debate about the causes of postnatal depression, but having a past history of depression has been shown to be a contributing factor.

If your partner experiences prolonged feelings like those listed below, it is a very good idea to get things checked out by your GP.
- feeling down;
- loss of interest or enjoyment in things;
- problems with appetite;
- difficulties getting to sleep;
- feeling exhausted, even months after the birth;

- crying, feeling irritable, anxious or confused;
- having panic attacks;
- loss of interest in sex;
- not wanting to go out or see people.

As mentioned, if your partner is exhibiting signs of depression, a doctor or health worker who knows about this stuff should see her promptly. There are practical things you can do to relieve some of the pressure on her. Get her some domestic help, or take on more of the housework and baby care yourself. Give your partner regular time to get a good rest.

NOTE: If you feel your partner poses a threat to herself, the baby or others, get her to your local hospital.

Postpartum Bleeding

As mentioned on page 182 under 'Vaginal Bleeding', a certain amount of bleeding is to be expected in the days after giving birth. However, any heavy bleeding, especially if accompanied

Why Do Babies Have Blue Eyes?

No matter what the eye colour inherited from the parents, most babies will be born with blue eyes. The reason for this is that melanin, the pigment responsible for eye, hair and skin colour, hasn't yet been deposited in the iris or darkened by exposure to ultraviolet light.

The amount of melanin a baby receives is coded through its parents' genes. Very small amounts of melanin produce blue or light-grey eyes, bigger amounts produce green, grey or light-brown eyes, while a lot of melanin produces black or brown eyes.

Production of melanin kicks in during the first year of a newborn's life, and eye colour is usually determined by six months. After adolescence, however, eye colour can start fading (along with everything else!), due to ageing.

Interestingly, new research in 2008 at the University of Copenhagen suggests that all people with blue eyes have a common ancestor and that the mutation for blue eyes only occurred about 6000 to 10000 years ago; prior to that it did not exist. The researchers tracked a mutation in blue-eyed people's genes which in effect switched off the ability to produce brown eyes.

by light-headedness, should be immediately investigated. It may be that your partner's uterus hasn't contracted properly following birth, or that there are ruptured blood vessels. Urgent medical attention will be required in this instance. (See 'Postpartum Haemorrhage', pages 163–164.)

Postpartum Infection

This means an infection in the womb or vagina following the birth of the baby. Postpartum infection can be a serious problem. If your partner has a fever, flu-like symptoms and/or unpleasant vaginal discharge following the birth of your baby, she may have a postpartum infection and will need to be checked out by a medical practitioner. Antibiotics and possible hospitalisation may be required.

Mastitis

Mastitis is an infection or inflammation of the breast. It's really painful, can make your partner sick and can cause problems with breastfeeding. It may be caused by nipple damage or by an oversupply of breast milk. Signs of mastitis include:

• painful, reddened areas of the breast;
• lumps in the breast;
• a fever or flu-like illness.

Treatment includes hand-expression of milk and antibiotics. Cool-packs applied to the breast may soothe it. Some women may require hospitalisation.

Basic Baby Care

It's a good idea not to leave all the baby care in the hands of your partner. Over the next year the relationship with your partner can be strained enough without her feeling resentful because you haven't helped with the baby (see 'Your Relationship With Your Partner', pages 206–208). Plus, if you ever want to have sex again, you'd better put in the hard yards with that baby now! So here are some basic tips and techniques you can use when attempting baby taming.

Swaddling

While every babe is different, generally newborn babies love being wrapped up tightly. If you think about it, for a large part of the time they spent in the womb they were packed in like John Holmes in budgie smugglers, so it makes sense that they like to feel swaddled. You may find that if they aren't wrapped they tend to wake or frighten themselves with the sudden involuntary movements of their arms.

Swaddling is also known as the ancient art of baby origami. Please see directions below.

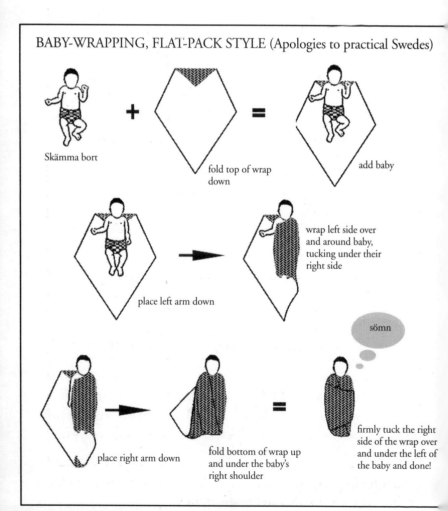

BABY-WRAPPING, FLAT-PACK STYLE (Apologies to practical Swedes)

Skämma bort

fold top of wrap down

add baby

place left arm down

wrap left side over and around baby, tucking under their right side

sömn

place right arm down

fold bottom of wrap up and under the baby's right shoulder

firmly tuck the right side of the wrap over and under the left of the baby and done!

Nappies

To cloth or not to cloth, that is the question. Regardless of your cloth- or disposable-nappy game plan, it is generally handy to have a few cloth nappies knocking about (if you don't use them as nappies they are great for wiping up baby vomit!). Baby origami continues with cloth-nappy folding. Just follow the simple directions shown below.

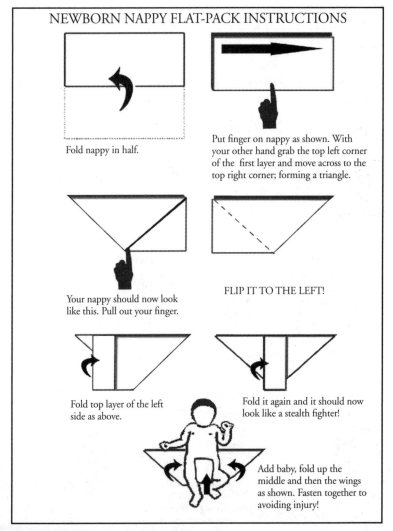

NEWBORN NAPPY FLAT-PACK INSTRUCTIONS

Fold nappy in half.

Put finger on nappy as shown. With your other hand grab the top left corner of the first layer and move across to the top right corner; forming a triangle.

Your nappy should now look like this. Pull out your finger.

FLIP IT TO THE LEFT!

Fold top layer of the left side as above.

Fold it again and it should now look like a stealth fighter!

Add baby, fold up the middle and then the wings as shown. Fasten together to avoiding injury!

But folding nappies is only the half of it. What you do with a spoiled nappy is another matter altogether.

Dressing and Bedding

This is often a hard one, as the little tacker can't talk to tell you what shade of pastel he/she would like to wear today, or whether it's to be Pumpkin Patch or Baby Esprit. Jokes aside, as a general rule of thumb your little one needs one more layer than you are wearing in order to stay comfortably warm. So, if you're bouncing about in a T-shirt and jeans, there's no need to wrap your baby up like the Michelin Man. Just think extra layer and pop a singlet under their T.

The same goes with bedding. If you are warm enough with a sheet, the baby will be warm enough with a sheet and a light blanket (see 'Sudden Infant Death Syndrome', page 203).

Communication and Babies

Babies are complex social creatures that need adults to survive. As such, they have a range of communication abilities that expand with growth in time. Following is a rough guide to baby's communication in the first year.

What a Baby Understands	
Age bracket	**Baby's response**
0–3 months	• Responds to sudden loud noises • Will be settled by familiar voices
3–6 months	• Responds to sounds by turning head towards source of sound • Recognises and responds to own name • Able to discriminate between emotion in voices
6–9 months	• Responds to 'no' by pausing • Recognises the names of family members • Able to participate in simple games like 'peek-a-boo' and 'round and round the garden' • Able to shake head for 'no' • Imitates actions of others
9–12 months	• Acts on simple verbal requests ('Get Daddy's beer!') • Understands simple questions ('Where is my beer?') • Waves/claps on verbal cue ('Yay, Daddy's got his beer!') • Enjoys songs and music

Language Acquisition

Almost all human beings are fluent in a language (sometimes more than one language) by the age of five, which is pretty amazing when you think about it. There are basically two overlapping schools of thought as to how we actually achieve this great feat. They involve the ideas of nature and nurture.

The first theory posits that children are able to absorb and reproduce more language than they are actually exposed to, so there must be some innate map of language in all of us in order for this to happen. Like bees being pre-programmed to build a hive from birth, the theory goes that buried in our genes is some kind of 'universal map' of grammar, and no matter what language is spoken this map gives the basic rules and patterns of language – even those that have not been specifically taught.

The second school of thought involves usage and experience of language in a child and believes that adults play an important role in the acquisition of language by speaking to children in a slow, grammatically obvious and repetitive way, which 'teaches' the language to the child.

Most linguists accept that both nature and nurture play a part in language learning; however, to what extent is still open for debate. There have been a number of interesting observations of deaf people which have contributed to the debate.

Professor Susan Goldin-Meadow of the University of Chicago studied two sets of deaf children in Taiwan and the United States and discovered that they developed a sign language not similar to their native English and Taiwanese, as would be expected, but with more in common to each other. The fact that grammatical patterns and word orders were more related to each other than to their native language seemed to suggest an in-built system at work.

Another intriguing example of language acquisition came from the deaf community in Nicaragua in the 1970s. At the time there was no formal sign language for deaf people in Nicaragua, and deaf children communicated with their non-deaf families with basic gestures. In 1977 a special education program was started and hundreds of previously isolated deaf people came together in special deaf schools.

What happened next was totally unexpected. The deaf children quickly established a complex sign language out of thin air, showing an innate ability to form language. Interestingly, deaf adults did not acquire the new language, suggesting that although language may be 'hard-wired' there is most likely a critical age to access it.

Babies May Learn Language in the Womb

A study conducted by the Max Planck Institute in Leipzig, Germany, suggests that babies may actually start learning the basics of language while still in the womb. Scientists compared 30 French and 30 German infants aged between two and five days old and found that the intonation of their cries differed.

The German babies' cries had a falling intonation while the French had a rising tone. The scientists speculate that the differing tones are related to the differing languages of French and German, which have mostly rising intonations and falling intonations respectively. The theory being that the babies pick this up while 'listening' in the womb.

What a Baby Says	
Age bracket	**Baby's response**
0–3 months	• Frequent crying • Looks at speaker's face when spoken to • Talks in goos, coos, gurgles and babbles … the height of witty conversation!
3–6 months	• Babbling increases • Exploration of single sounds, like 'ba', 'da' and 'ma' • Chats insensibly when spoken to, or talks to favoured objects • Understands and responds to simple words like 'up' • Initiates social interaction by smiling or babbling to get attention
6–9 months	• Combines two or more sounds, like 'mama', 'dada' • Starts to imitate sounds of speech • Uses simple gestures, like hitting daddy in the face for 'no', or waving goodbye
9–12 months	• Names some objects, even ones that are out of sight ('So, sweetie, where is Daddy's mobile?') • Will point to indicate object ('Over there, Dad, in the bin!') • Increased imitation of words and language

Sleep and Babies

The amount of rest you get over the next six months depends largely on the amount of sleep the baby gets, or on the goodwill of your partner. Fortunately babies need a lot of sleep – they have heaps of growing to do, so when they aren't eating they are

THE GREAT COMMUNICATOR

Baby's firsts	Baby's age (months)

....

....

Babbles

....

Squeals

....

Smiles

....

Says 'Mama'

....

Says 'Dada'

....

Say 'no'

....

Waves bye-bye

....

Points

....

Other significant milestones:

....

....

....

....

resting. As a baby gets older its sleep patterns change. Following is a rough guide to a baby's sleep needs as it grows.

Newborns: six to eight sleeps a day, each lasting 2–3 hours;

6 weeks to 3 months: four to five sleeps a day, each lasting 2½–3 hours;

4 to 4½ months: two longer sleeps (4–5 hours), one usually at night, and three shorter sleeps (2–2½ hours each);

4½ to 6 months: 8–10 hours at night (with a feed in that time) plus two to three daytime sleeps (2½ hours each).

Signs of Tiredness, and How to Settle a Baby

Ah, grasshopper, recognise the seven signs of baby tiredness!

- grimacing;
- yawning;
- grizzling;
- frowning crying;
- sucking;
- clenching fists;
- crying.

   When you observe any of these signs of tiredness, prepare your baby for sleep. General preparations should include:

- check your baby's nappy. (It's hard to sleep coated in poo!);
- swaddle, if your baby likes to be swaddled;
- put into bed as per SIDS guidelines (see 'Sudden Infant Death Syndrome', page 203).

More specific settling techniques for different age groups are as follows:

Newborn to 3 months:

- if the baby is quiet, allow to settle. If crying, cuddle or gently pat until calmer;
- try talking/singing to your baby to help with settling, but don't maintain eye contact;
- leave your baby for a brief time to see if he/she will settle;
- if your baby is still crying, go in and comfort him/her, then leave again. You may have to do this several times;
- if your baby wakes in under one hour, try to resettle him/her.

Babies' Sense of Self and Time

Anecdotal wisdom has it that babies do not possess self-consciousness up until the age of about two or three.

The general view is that babies feel more a part of their direct family until this time. This observation was put to the test in the 1970s when researchers got a bunch of babies and infants, put lipstick on their noses and put a mirror in front of them.

The results were that most six- to 12-month-olds thought their reflection was another baby and didn't try to wipe the lipstick off; after 12 months reactions differed, with a large percentage showing wariness and withdrawal or self-admiration and embarrassment; and 65 per cent of 20- to 24-month-olds clearly recognised themselves and tried to touch the lipstick on their noses.

It has been suggested that this self-recognition may explain the so-called 'terrible twos', a time when infants become rather irritable and are prone to throwing tantrums. It is thought that the sudden mental separation from the family and the newly discovered fact that they are their own entity may be the cause for self-centred behaviour.

A similar experiment by Daniel Povinelli at the University of Louisiana in 1996 attempted to work out a baby's sense of time and being. Povinelli's team wanted to pinpoint the exact age at which children get an 'autobiographical' knowledge of themselves. (Povinelli didn't see the mirror experiment as evidence of understanding self but perhaps more a case of recognising a bunch of features labelled as 'me'.)

The team's experiment involved videoing children playing a game and then showing them the video a short time later. While taking the video, one of the experimenters would give the child a reassuring pat on the head and in doing so surreptitiously plant a large, brightly coloured sticker on the child's head. The idea was that if the child watching the video reached up to see if the sticker was still on his or her head, that child had a sense that 'they' were 'them', so to speak, and were also able to connect the past to the present rather than living in the moment.

The results were that none of the two-year-olds and only 25 per cent of three-year-olds reached up to touch their heads. In contrast, 75 per cent of the study's four-year-olds looked for the sticker. Povinelli suggested that the experiment showed the phenomenon of 'infantile amnesia', which is the term used to explain our general lack of memory up to the age of about three.

3 months to 6 months:

- if the baby is quiet, allow him/her to settle. If crying, leave the room and allow him/her the opportunity to settle by himself/herself;
- your baby may initially be upset when you leave the room. Wait a few minutes. If your baby is still crying, go in and offer brief comfort, then leave again;
- if your baby continues to be upset, return and offer comfort until he/she calms. Then leave the room to allow them to self-settle. (This may take some time!)

NOTE: Things that may calm your bub include cuddling, rhythmical movement, walking or rocking, baby massage, a relaxing bath (for the baby!), playing music (avoid Megadeath or White Snake), a dummy, a drink of cooled boiled water. How you settle your baby is your personal choice, and we advise that you mix and match and work out what suits both baby and you.

Some babies are little buggers when it comes to settling. There are experts (like the Tresillian organisation – see 'Useful Contacts', page 210) who run daytime courses or even overnight residential care to help you teach your baby how to sleep. Contact your community health centre for details, or ring the hotline number.

There are three reasons for breastfeeding: the milk is always at the right temperature; it comes in attractive containers; and the cat can't get it.

Irena Chalmers

Crying

While it may not seem like it at the time, babies always cry for a reason. Go through the following list to work out why the little tacker is making all the fuss, and remember: if you are losing your patience with a crying baby, put the tiny foghorn down in a safe place and walk away for a moment to collect yourself.

Possible causes for crying:
- Is the baby hungry or thirsty?
- Is the baby too hot or too cold?
- Does the baby need a nappy change?
- Do you think the baby has pain or feels unwell?
- Could the baby be feeling scared?
- Is the baby over-tired?

NOTE: If you really can't work out what's happening with an inconsolable baby, it's worthwhile getting them checked out by a doctor or by your local hospital's emergency department.

Feeding Babies

Human babies were designed to feed from human breasts, but in some instances breastfeeding isn't an option for women and/ or their babies. Maternal illness or an insufficient milk supply,

Breastfed Babies Make Better Teens

In yet another coup for the pro-breastfeeding lobby, the ABC news website cited an extensive study published in the *Journal of Paediatrics* in 2010 claimed that breastfeeding leads to better behaviour in the dreaded teen years.

The study followed about 3000 women in Western Australia and tracked their little sandgropers through to early adolescence. The women included in the study had employed a range of feeding practices, from complete bottle-feeding to total breastfeeding, with breastfeeding being carried out for certain lengths of time. The results were startling.

The study found that the behaviour of breastfed babies as teens was markedly better than their bottle-fed counterparts. Interestingly, for each additional month that a child was breastfed, behaviour in teenagers improved.

Professor Sven Silburn, one of the authors of the study, concluded that, 'we can say clearly that breastfeeding for six months or longer is positively associated with mental health and wellbeing in children and adolescents'.

So, if you want to avoid a day at court chaperoning your teen on shoplifting charges, then try and get them on the breast.

or a baby unwilling (or unable) to take the breast, may on some occasions make bottle-feeding a necessity. Then there are those women or couples who consider bottle-feeding more convenient. Others again may choose to combine breast- and bottle-feeding.

Breastfeeding

Breast is best, there is no denying it. Breast milk has the energy, hormones and protein tailored to meet the needs of the human infant.

He Doesn't Look Like the Postman

New mothers, it seems, will relate the softly formed features of their newborn to your ugly mug no matter how dissimilar they actually are. Evolution plays a part in this scenario, with a research team from the University of Montpellier in France claiming that it's basically all to do with the male ego.

The research, conducted in 2007, asked the parents of 83 children under the age of six, from 69 families, to rate their offspring's resemblance to their mother or father. The catch was that 209 unrelated judges, with photos of the same families, did the same.

An amazing 100 per cent of mothers surveyed said that their boys looked like the father, with 77 per cent saying their daughters had the same Dad-like features in the first three days after birth. Between eight months and 22 months the figure dropped slightly to an 86 per cent recognition for boys and 72 per cent recognition rate for girls. Furthermore, eight out of 10 of the men in the study thought that their child looked like them.

The independent judges, on the other hand, claimed that 50 per cent of the kids looked like their mum and a third looked like their dad. Photos of the postman were not included.

The upshot of all this seems to be that mums, on a subconscious level, will pretty much always say that their baby looks like their husband in order to allay his fears about the paternity of the child. This bio-evolutionary trait, the researchers concluded, ensures that the father, convinced that the child is his, will take a more active role in looking after the newborn and its mother.

Advantages for babies are:
- it gives them the complete nutrients and fluid they need for the first six months of life;
- it protects them from some illnesses, like diarrhoea, and other longer-term things like heart disease and diabetes;
- it helps their jaws to develop properly.

Advantages for your partner are:
- it helps your partner get into shape quicker (milk production takes heaps of energy);
- evidence has shown women who breastfeed may reduce the risk of developing breast cancer and other illnesses, such as type-2 diabetes;
- it requires no preparation and is fully portable;
- it costs nothing.

You can help your partner when she is breastfeeding by:
- making sure she is comfortable;
- making sure she has a drink beside her (breastfeeding is thirsty work!);
- making sure she is getting enough rest;
- being supportive if she has problems establishing feeding.

Expressing Breast Milk

You guys want to go for a long-awaited romantic dinner but your partner is worried about not being around to breastfeed the baby … Don't worry, she can remove some of her milk, put it in a bottle and use it for later: it's called expressing! There are a range of manual methods, plus hand and electric pumps, available for this purpose. Electric pumps can be hired from chemists. You can store the breast milk in your fridge for three to five days (4°C or lower). Store it in the back of the refrigerator where it is coldest. If you are freezing breast milk you can keep it for three months in a normal separate door freezer or 6–12 months in a deep freezer (-18°C or lower). NOTE: Once frozen milk has been thawed you must discard it within 24 hours and never refreeze!

Diet While Breastfeeding

You are what you eat or is it your baby is what your partner eats? Anyway having a good balanced diet is essential during breastfeeding. Alcohol while breastfeeding is a no-no as it will be present in the breast milk. If your partner wants a girls night out she will need to express and discard the alcohol-tainted milk. There is anecdotal evidence that spicy food can cause tummy upsets in a newborn so get her to lay off the laksa as well.

Bottle-feeding

If your partner has decided, for whatever reason, to bottle-feed, be prepared to cop some flak from friends and relatives. But remember, it's not their decision: you have to make the choice that is right for you.

There are advantages to bottle-feeding. In the first place, anyone can babysit, and in the second place, *you* can get up at four o'clock in the morning to feed the baby … yay! If your partner does decide to bottle-feed, it's important she gets some advice from her caregiver about how to suppress breastfeeding.

Formula

'Formula' is the name given to a cow- or soy-based powdered milk product which has been supplemented with various vitamins and minerals in an attempt to imitate human breast milk. There are various brands of formula available, and all must meet the Australian food and safety standards. Different formulas are available for differing stages of a baby's development. See your chemist or talk with your caregiver for advice. (NOTE: The most expensive brands aren't necessarily better for the baby.)

If your family is riddled with people who suffer from allergies, and if you have decided to formula-feed your baby, discuss this with your caregiver or chemist. The formula you choose may help reduce the bub's risk of becoming an anaphylactic (allergic) catastrophe, too!

What You Will Need for Bottle-feeding

Bottle-feeding necessitates keeping bottles scrupulously clean, so in addition to the bottles themselves you are going to need to set yourself up with some sterilising equipment. The following list sets out the requirements:
• 2–6 large baby bottles, with teats, caps and teat covers;
• a bottle brush to clean the bottles;
• sterilising equipment (a microwave steriliser, or a sterilising

To Snip or Not to Snip

Circumcision is the surgical practice of cutting off some or all of the foreskin from the male penis, usually just after birth. The practice is often done for religious and cultural reasons, or because the parents assert that there may be some health advantages to the child.

Both Jews and Muslims practise circumcision according to their religious beliefs, while in some Aboriginal tribes circumcision is performed as a ritual at the age of 12 or 13, as a transition to manhood. Aboriginal circumcision is customarily done (cross your legs now!) without anaesthetic, using a cutting implement such as a sharpened stone or shell. Sub-incision, the actual cutting of the undersurface of the penis where the urethra is slit open lengthways, is also practised at the age of 16 or 17 by some tribes.

Historian Robert Darby reports that the practice of circumcision rose sharply in Australia between 1910 and 1920 because of fears of the contraction of syphilis during World War I. The rate of circumcisions then peaked at about 85 per cent in the mid-1950s, before falling back again to 50 per cent by 1975, and only 10 per cent by 1995.

Darby asserts that the original catalyst for the practice came from Victorian England, where religious piety, coupled with a morbid fear of masturbation, caused reason to believe that the removal of the foreskin would prevent excessive stimulation of the area and prevent the supposedly fatal (but imaginary) disease 'spermatorrhoea' (a condition caused by the loss of sperm through anything other than heterosexual intercourse).

Arguments For Circumcision

Those in the pro-circumcision camp believe that the chances of contracting a multitude of diseases can be minimised by the removal of the foreskin. These diseases or potentially preventable health problems include serious kidney infections in infancy, sexually transmitted diseases, including human immunodeficiency (HIV) infections, chlamydia infection and human papilloma virus (HPV) in young men, and invasive cancer of the penis in middle and old age.

Arguments Against Circumcision

Beyond believing the practice of circumcision to be painful and 'barbaric', those in the anti-circumcision camp argue that the advantages of keeping the foreskin far outweigh the minor risk of disease contraction as promoted by those in the pro-circumcision camp.

Some of the arguments for keeping the foreskin include the belief that it provides protection to the penis in the early stages of life, and that sexual sensitivity may be decreased with its removal.

solution and bucket to soak, or a large saucepan in which to boil the bottles and other bits).

NOTE: Teats have different-sized holes that determine the speed of feeding: the bigger the hole, the faster the flow! So make sure to ask your chemist to help you get the right teat for your bub.

How to Prepare a Bottle

It's not rocket science, gents, but it's a bit of a process. Here's what you have to do:

- wash your hands;
- use boiled water to add to the formula (make sure to let it cool!);
- measure the required amount of water;
- add the required amount of formula as per the manufacturer's instructions;
- seal and shake;
- warm on the stovetop to feed to the hungry tacker (don't make it too hot!).

General Tips When Feeding with a Bottle

Whether using formula or expressed breast milk, keep in mind the following points when feeding a baby by bottle:

- it takes about 20–40 minutes to bottle-feed a baby. Don't rush it!;
- don't use a microwave to heat a baby's bottle – it can heat unevenly, causing burning;
- check the temperature by shaking a little formula or breast milk from the bottle onto your wrist. If it feels hot on your skin, it's too hot! Leave it to cool for a while;
- don't prop a bottle in your baby's mouth and go off to make a coffee. Leaving your baby unattended while feeding can result in choking;
- halfway through a feed and after a feed is finished, burp the baby. This involves sitting the child upright and rubbing his or her back until they burp. Actually, just sitting them upright is often all that's necessary;
- throw out any made-up formula after 24 hours (old milk can make babies sick!). Be sure to follow the manufacturer's guidelines;

- throw out any expressed breast milk that has been in the refrigerator longer than three to five days.

Possible Serious Baby Stuff to Worry About

Sorry to say but there are some serious things that can go wrong with your little bub. But now you're a father get used to it. You are probability going to a little worried for your kid(s) for the rest of your life. It goes hand in hand with love.

Sudden Infant Death Syndrome (SIDS)

You'd have to have been living under a rock not to have heard about Sudden Infant Death Syndrome (SIDS). Since safe sleeping practices have been put in place, SIDS deaths have fallen markedly.

To help keep your little one safe, the following guidelines and sleeping arrangements are recommended by the SIDS organisation:

- position your baby on its back for sleeping (the risk of SIDS is increased if babies sleep on their tummies);
- tuck in your baby's bed clothes securely;
- make sure your baby's head remains uncovered during sleep;
- make up the bassinette/cot so that the baby's feet are positioned at the foot of the bed;
- quilts, doonas, pillows, soft toys and cot bumpers in the cot are not recommended;
- use a firm, clean, well-fitting mattress;
- do not put your baby on a waterbed or beanbag;
- avoid smoking near your baby;
- don't share a bed with your baby – the baby may slip under the bedding or into a pillow, become trapped between the bed and a parent or the wall, fall out of bed, overheat from too much bedding, or a sleeping parent may roll on him/her. And of course, don't bed-share if you have been drinking alcohol or are affected by other drugs.

Jaundice

This is a yellow discolouration of your newborn's skin and eyes as a result of the breakdown or red blood cells or of an intestinal blockage of some kind. Depending on the cause and the severity of jaundice, some babies can become lethargic, not want to feed and may need further care in hospital. With the most common type of jaundice for babies (the blood breakdown type), the yellow skin and eye colour is caused by a substance called bilirubin. If your baby needs to be treated in hospital, it will be placed under lights to break down the bilirubin. This is known as phototherapy.

Recessive Gene Explained

Ever wondered why some babies pop out with red hair or blue eyes while their parents are of black-haired, brown-eyed persuasion? Then you should have been listening in class while your biology teacher was ranting on about phenotypes and recessive genes, rather than looking out the window or at that girl walking down the street.

So here we go again. Genes are present in the cells of all living things and act as the 'recipe' of what the plant or animal looks like, how it will survive and how it will interact with its environment. These genes are strung along long strands of material called chromosomes. In most living things, including humans, pairs of chromosomes make up a double helix strand called DNA. One chromosome is from the mother and one from the father. Humans have 23 pairs of these chromosomes, while a fruit fly only has four.

In the case of red or blonde hair and blue eyes, these characteristics (or phenotypes) are represented by a recessive gene, while black or brown hair and brown eyes are represented by a dominant gene.

So, each person carries two genes for eye and hair colour, yet for a recessive trait to be expressed in the parents' offspring, both parents must be carrying at least one of the recessive genes for these traits.

If both parents have brown eyes, for example, and both carry a recessive gene for red hair, then there is a one in four chance that their child will be a redhead.

Recessive traits are rarer than dominant ones in most populations, with blonde hair, in particular, thought to be present in only about 2 per cent of the world population. No wonder they have so much fun.

Back at the Crib … With a Crib

Your partner is fine and your baby is fine. Your caregivers give you a weary wave from the closing hospital door … you are on your own. You put your baby into the travel capsule and with your amazing partner at your side you head home. Once you get there life is not going to be the same and sorry to say you might feel a bit at sea. Don't worry buddy, you will pull through and to help you along here are a few tips. Good luck!

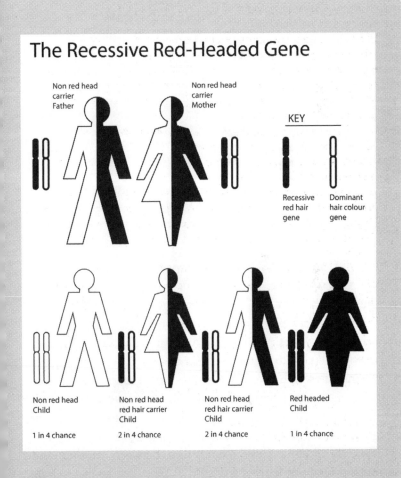

The Recessive Red-Headed Gene

Non red head
carrier
Father

Non red head
carrier
Mother

KEY

Recessive
red hair
gene

Dominant
hair colour
gene

Non red head
Child

1 in 4 chance

Non red head
red hair carrier
Child

2 in 4 chance

Non red head
red hair carrier
Child

2 in 4 chance

Red headed
Child

1 in 4 chance

What to Do With the Placenta

Some folk do some trippy things with the placenta – bury them under trees, cook them with onions or keep them in their freezers … but hey, what takes place between consenting adults is cool, right?

It has been suggested by some that eating the placenta can reduce the incidence of postnatal depression and replace the much-needed nutrients that have been lost during the childbirth process. Others dismiss these claims, saying that there is no link between a non-placenta diet and postnatal depression, and that for a well-nourished woman there is no medical justification for eating the placenta at all.

It's your choice. The following recipe has been included for the braver among you.

Placenta With Polenta

for the polenta
400 ml water
pinch of salt
200 g polenta
1 large knob of butter
50 g parmesan cheese, grated

for the placenta
50 g butter
100 g bacon, diced
300 g placenta, cut in 5 mm
   slices
1 small bunch sage

for the chanterelles
olive oil
1 clove of garlic, sliced
1 small bunch parsley, chopped
200 g chanterelle mushrooms,
   trimmed and brushed
salt and pepper, to taste
a squeeze of lemon
knob of butter, extra

Your Relationship With Your Partner

This is somewhat of a bitter pill to swallow, but you need to recognise in the first few weeks after getting the baby home that your partner's physical and emotional needs are far more important than yours. She is going to be tired and sleep-deprived and needs to be looked after.

Having a new baby is a bit of an emotional roller-coaster ride. Both you and your partner might be apprehensive about caring for the baby, be tired and stressed about the future, so a bit of disagreement is probably inevitable.

There is often a close relationship between mother and newborn which sometimes leaves the man feeling like a lone shag on the proverbial rock. However, if you're helpful to your partner, get involved in the care of the little one and make time

To make the polenta, bring the water to a boil in a large saucepan, add the salt and whisk in the polenta until the mixture is very thick. Cook gently for 20–30 minutes, stirring frequently with a wooden spoon, until the polenta comes away from the sides of the pan. Turn out onto a plate and leave to cool and set.

Preheat the grill to hot. Cut the polenta into slices and grill, ensuring both sides have a crispy skin. Rub with the butter and sprinkle with the grated parmesan.

For the placenta, melt half the butter in a heavy saucepan, add the bacon and fry until crispy. Remove the bacon and drain off any excess fat. Add the remaining butter and, when it foams, add the placenta and sage. Cook the placenta slices for 3 minutes each side. Just before serving, return the bacon to the pan to warm through.

For the chanterelles, heat a heavy-based frying pan and add a dash of olive oil. Add the garlic and parsley, then the chanterelles, and season with salt and pepper. Cook until the chanterelles have a light golden colour, and finish with a squeeze of lemon.

Finally, rub the polenta fingers with more butter and arrange the chanterelles over them. Serve with the placenta and bacon on the side.

to do things as a couple (without the baby!), you can keep your relationship strong. Remember, though, that if your relationship hits rock bottom, get some help! There are organisations out there that can provide counselling and support for relationship issues (see 'Useful Contacts', page 210).

When Can We Have Sex Again?
There is no hard-and-fast rule about when you can have sex after the baby; it just shouldn't cause harm or pain to your partner. This will depend on how the labour and birth went. (She may have had vaginal tearing, which will take some weeks to heal.) Your caregiver might have an opinion, so discuss it with them. Just don't jump her as soon as she's put the baby in the cot at home for the first time! Your partner may be sleep-deprived and

generally out of sorts, so be considerate when attempting to be amorous with your loved one.

Birth Control

Unless you both have made the decision to have babies in quick succession (and you would have to be mad!), before you have sex again you'll need to sort out some kind of birth control. Breastfeeding offers a sort of natural immunity against getting pregnant, but it's definitely not foolproof.

Movin' On ...

OK, Big Daddy, it's up to you now. Start working on those bad jokes, and nurture an attitude of calm among the chaos. Most of all, enjoy!

Useful Contacts

Breastfeeding Support

Australian Breastfeeding Association (AUS)
www.breastfeeding.asn.au
Tel: 1800 6862 686
Provides web-based information and a telephone advice service for breastfeeding mothers.

Breastfeeding.com (USA)
www.breastfeeding.com
An American website that provides breastfeeding information and more.

Contraception

FPA Family Planning (NSW)
www.fpansw.org.au
Tel: 02 8252 4300
Provides web-based information about contraception and a telephone service for folk in NSW.

Community Health Centres (Check Your Local Phone Directory)

These centres provide a range of free health services for your new family.

Immunisation

Immunise Australia Program (AUS
www.immunise.health.gov.au
Provides information and contacts for all things immunisation.

Postnatal Depression
Beyond Blue (AUS)
www.beyondblue.org.au
Tel: 1300 224 636
An excellent web-based resource for information and contacts
for postnatal depression.

Baby Settling
Tresillian (NSW)
Tel: 02 9787 0855 (Sydney); 1800 637 357 (elsewhere in NSW)
Provides a range of baby care advise for new parents.

Tweddle Early Parenting Advice (VIC)
Tel: 03 9689 1577
Provides support for parents in the early years.

Relationship Assistance
Relationships Australia (AUS)
www.relationships.com.au
Tel: 1300 364 277
Offer a range of services to help maintain a strong healthy
relationship with your partner.

SIDS Advice and Bereavement Counselling
SIDS and Kids (AUS)
www.sidsandkids.org
Tel: 1300 308 307
Offers web-based safe sleeping advice and state
contacts for bereavement counselling.

Acknowlegements

We would like to acknowledge Sonal and Katina, our long-suffering partners, who rued the day they'd ever mentioned our 'lack of interest' in pregnancy, but nonetheless were very helpful in their bottomless wisdom and suggestions for the book. Thanks also to Katina for providing some of the graphics. Maya, Odin, Ada, Lilli, Isaak, whose dads' neglect and selfish literary commitments may have scarred them for life. Ms Kate Griew, midwife extraordinaire who made many kind and helpful suggestions. Sean and Magda (and now Fin), who road-tested a few early chapters and came back with some great constructive criticism. All our friends for putting up with us crapping on about 'the book'. Jacinta for seeing its potential. Helen from Hachette Australia for her 'hot' cover idea and taking a risk, and our ever-diplomatic editors, Susan Gray and Kate Ballard.

A Note on Sources

We would like to thank: Diane M Fraser and Margaret A Cooper for their *Myles' Textbook for Midwives, Fifteenth Edition* (Elsevier Limited, Edinburgh, 2009) – we used this well-loved text to check a lot of those rusty facts that were hiding somewhere in the recesses of Jon's midwifery mind; the hard-working team (Murray W Enkin, Marc J N C Keirse, James P Neilson, Caroline A Crowther, Lelia Dudley, Ellen D Hodnett and G Justus Hofmeyr) who put together *A Guide to Effective Care in Pregnancy and Childbirth, Third Edition* (Oxford University Press, Oxford, 2000) – this wonderful guide provided evidence for some of the care suggested by our book; when we were stumped by a question of pregnancy-related physiology, we turned to the fantastic *Physiology in Childbearing with Anatomy and Related Biosciences, Second Edition* (Ballière Tindall, Oxford, 2004) by those loveable ladies of science, Dot Stables and Jean Rankin; finally to Dr Pieter van Dongen for his article 'Caesarean Section – Etymology and Early History', published in the *South African Journal of Obstetrics and Gynaecology*, August 2009, which provided a lot of the information used in 'Caesareans: Myths and Milestones.' Thanks Doc!

Stephen Mitchell teaches writing at the University of Technology, Sydney. He has a background in graphic design, publishing and education and frequently comes up with crazy ideas like, 'I know, let's write a book about pregnancy for men!', some of which actually come to fruition. He is also a man and a father, making him well qualified to co-author a book about pregnancy for men. He lives in Sydney with his wife and daughter.

Jon Farry is a registered nurse and midwife who currently lives in the Kimberley, Western Australia. He has spent much of his working life drinking too much coffee in various emergency departments in New South Wales, and completed his midwifery training at Sydney's Royal Prince Alfred Hospital, in 2007. Now he works as a nurse/midwife in retrieval medicine for the Royal Flying Doctor Service. He currently lives with his partner Katina and their lovely children.

Index

postnatal care 39, 43, 183
postnatal depression 185–6, 206, 210
postpartum haemorrhage (PPH) 160, 163–4, 167, 170, 182, 186–7
postpartum infection 166, 187
pram 119
pre-eclampsia 108, 168
Pre-eclampsia Foundation (USA) 108
pregnancy 24, 33
  care during 36, 38–9
  caregivers 33, 40, 44–5, 66–7, 152–4
  checklist 31
  first trimester 49–75
  regional services 47
  second trimester 77–109
  symptoms 23–5
  testing 25
  third trimester 111–39
pre-term birth 70, 87, 103, 104, 131, 132–3
private hospital care 40–1, 45–7
progesterone 23, 91, 92, 93, 94, 124, 125
prolactin 91
prostaglandin 135–6, 138, 149
psychiatric problems 68
public hospitals 45–7
  midwifery-led care 43, 44
  private obstetric care 40–1

public patients 41–3
  shared-care GP 43–4
puerperal fever 145
puerperium 181
pulmonary embolism 68, 170
pushing 157–8, 159

Quit (AUS) 28

recessive genes 204, 205
red hair 205
red lentil curry labour soup 137
relationships 206–7
Relationships Australia (AUS) 29, 210
relax-and-see approach to conception 3, 5
relaxation 21, 96, 133, 151
relaxin 91, 92, 93
reproductive cycle 6–8
  chemical pollutants 15
Rhesus factor 65, 100, 103, 168
rights, knowing your 34, 42
rituals 155
Royal Australian and New Zealand College of Obstetricians and Gynaecologists (AUS & NZ) 48
Royal Women's Hospital (VIC) 75
rubella immune status 66
rupture of membranes 135, 148
  pre-term 131